Chicheŵa
for English Speakers

A New &
Simplified
Approach

Nathaniel Maxson

**Chicheŵa for English Speakers -
a New and Simplified Approach**
Copyright © Nathaniel Maxson 2011.

978-1479378838

njmaxson@gmail.com
www.chichewagrammar.net

Cover design by Joel Designs
http://joeldesigns.prowebmalawi.com

Chicheŵa for English Speakers

Introduction

Chicheŵa is an important language in Southern Africa. In Malaŵi, it is the national language and the mother tongue of a large part of the population. Zambia hosts Chicheŵa's close cousin, Chinyanja, as an important trade language. Chicheŵa speakers can be found in Mozambique, Zimbabwe, and, in smaller numbers, in South Africa.

Malaŵian culture, especially, is intrinsically bound up in the language of Chicheŵa. In social life, culture, religion, and all other areas, the Chicheŵa language fills in color to the tapestry of Malaŵian life. This is true even in the cities, although some people are now replacing Chicheŵa with English as their standard medium of formal communication.

As a visitor or expatriate worker in Malaŵi, any knowledge of Chicheŵa goes a long way toward laying a foundation for good communications, and an obvious effort in that direction is almost universally well appreciated.

Chicheŵa is a Bantu language along with many of the other languages in Sub-Saharan Africa. A characteristic of the Bantu languages is that the words in the language are built from basic building blocks of syllables that have various meanings. Another characteristic of Chicheŵa, along with its Bantu sister languages, is that it uses a system of 'concordial' prefixes to show agreement between nouns and all the words connected to that noun. These and various other factors make Chicheŵa – believe it or not – a simple and relatively easy language to learn!

This book is an effort on my part to make that true for you. It is not designed to be an exhaustive treatment of the grammatical details of the Chicheŵa language. You will find that there are some things missing. Nor is this course a textbook that you should attempt to use exclusively by itself. Rather, this book is intended to be an aid to those who are already or soon to be exposed to the Chicheŵa language being spoken by real Malaŵians. It will be especially useful to those who are learning the language in the environment of everyday life. Use this book as a commentary on the language to try to help unravel some of the mystery that may seem to surround all the strange sounds and phrases!

Each chapter is focused on one major grammatical theme. The text is written in an easy to read style, especially in the earlier chapters, to encourage you to read all the way through a chapter before stopping. After reading through a chapter, you should go over all the vocabulary and example sentences a couple of times to fix them in your mind.

After you have gone through a given chapter a sufficient number of times to have picked up the majority of the things presented in it, it is time to move on to the next chapter. After moving on, frequently come back and review each chapter to cement everything in your mind and tie it in with anything new you have learned.

Here is a pointer that helped me tremendously in my own language acquisition process: Try to get the big picture! If at all possible, forge ahead and expose yourself, though imperfectly, to the whole book and try to see how it all fits together in macro. Pick up major principles and try to see the 'structure' of the language. At the same time, keep going through the book slowly to get the details.

As a very important part of your language learning journey, find a competent Chicheŵa helper (or helpers) who can critique your pronunciation and usage! Believe me, a competent helper is worth more than all the books you can get!

For more language resources, visit me online at www.chichewagrammar.net.

A special thanks to Andrew Goodson of Kamuzu Academy for his thoughts, suggestions and encouragement. He kindly contributed a lot of advice and helped me make this book a success. In fact, the chapter entitled 'Tones' is almost entirely his material.

Steven Paas, author of the most comprehensive Chicheŵa dictionary in print, also was a great encouragement and inspiration. His third edition of *Dictionary Mtanthauziramawu* is due to be out in early 2012. This dictionary is a tool you must have as you pursue mastery of Chicheŵa. Get your own copy from bookstores across Malawi and Zambia. His website www.chichewadictionary.org also offers at-your-fingertips access to the dictionary database.

Chapter 1: Pronunciation

Chicheŵa pronunciation patterns are generally quite predictable, even if not so easy for English speakers. Be sure to go over these with a native speaker who can demonstrate the peculiarities of each sound. Note that the pronunciation comparisons written here are given from my perspective as an American English speaker.

Vowels:

Chicheŵa uses the five vowels a, e, i, o and u. One of the things you will have to guard against is the dipthong glide that we use on most of our English vowels. (Say, 'mine,' and see if you don't pronounce it as if there were two vowels [a + i] instead of one.) All vowels in Chicheŵa should be pronounced as simple, single vowels, without the gliding tendencies of English vowel pronunciation.

A – almost 'a' in 'father', not the 'a' in 'apple' or 'ate'
Aaa! – Sound of surprise or disbelief
ana – children

E – 'e' in 'buffet,' not quite the 'e' in 'egg'
Eee! – Yes
mchere – salt

I – 'i' in 'machine,' not as in 'is' or 'find'
Iii! – expression of response to something bad
phiri – mountain

O – 'o' in 'comb,' never like 'o' in 'hot', involves more emphatic lip shaping than English

zikomo – thank you, excuse me
odi – announcing arrival at a house, instead of knocking

U – 'oo' in 'tooth'; not 'u' in 'umbrella'; again more
emphatic lip shaping than English
munthu – person
buku – book

Double vowels:
Ntcheu (said like 'iN-tche-wu') – town in Malaŵi
mau (like 'ma-wu') – word

Voiced consonants:

'G' differs little from English.

galu	dog
gwafa	guava
gogo	grandparent

'J' is pronounced a little harder, almost 'dj,' but not quite.

aja   those
ujeni   such and such (spoken when trying to
think of the correct word or name!)
Jemusi   James

'M' and 'N' are similar to English.

mayi	mother
madzi	water
nambala	number

'V' is harder like 'bv'.
chivomezi   earthquake

kuvala	to wear

'W'

wina	another (person)

'Y'

yankho	answer

'Z'

zinthu	things

'B' and 'D'

These two are likely to give you trouble, as each of them has two forms, 'explosive' and 'implosive.' In English, we only use the 'explosive' form.

The 'implosive' form is pronounced by slightly sucking air into the mouth just before forming the sound and releasing the suction created. The 'explosive' form is the one you already know, where you form the sound as you expel air from your mouth.

The 'implosive' form is used when the letter is alone or with 'w' or 'y', whereas the 'explosive' form is used when the the letter occurs together with another consonant or in words borrowed from English.

Implosive:

Bola	Better
Bowa bwanga	My mushroom
Dengu	Basket
Diso	Eye

Explosive:

Bala	Bar
Dilesi	Dress
Mbale	Dish
Ndiwo	Relish

Voiceless consonants:

'P', 'K', 'T'

Here we encounter three letters that will trip you up if you are not careful. Each of these letters actually represents two different sounds, one aspirated and the other unaspirated. In the aspirated form the letter is pronounced with a puff of voiceless air, whereas the unaspirated form is pronounced 'softer' without the puff of air.

Interestingly enough, in English we also have aspirated and unaspirated forms for these letters, only that we write them in exactly the same way with no indication that the letter is aspirated or not. In English, aspirated forms are used whenever the letter k, p or t begins a word. Say a word like 'pop,' 'town,' or 'kite.' Notice the puff of air that accompanies the letter k, p, or t. Now notice the difference for these letters in words like 'spoon,' 'steal,' and 'skate.'

Fortunately for us, the aspirated forms are always written with an 'h' in Chicheŵa, while the unaspirated are written alone.

Khoma	Wall	(aspirated k)
Kukhoma	To hammer, hit	(first k not aspirated, but the second one is)
Phiri	Mountain	(aspirated p)
Thovu	Foam, lather, bubbles	(aspirated t)
Koma	But	(unaspirated)

Kukoma	To taste good, be nice (k's unaspirated)
Pitani bwino.	Go well. (unaspirated p)
Pirirani!	Keep going, don't lose heart! (unaspirated p)
Tate	Father (unaspirated t's)

Because of the fact that English uses aspirated versions of these consonants wherever the letter starts a word, you will have a particularly hard time pronouncing the unaspirated forms of these letters at the beginning of a word. As a clue, when pronouncing 'pitani', think of 'bitani' but still say 'p', 'dade' for 'tate' and still say 't', and 'gugoma' for 'kukoma' and still say 'k'!

Other voiceless consonants:
'Ch,' 'Tch'

| Chinthu | Thing (avoid saying 'tchinthu', Chicheŵa 'ch' is softer and smoother) |
| Tchire | Bush, wild area (pronounced very alike to English 'ch') |

'F' – similar to English

| Fikani! | (You) arrive, come! |

'H' – similar to English

| Hema | Tent |

Nasalised sounds:
'M' and 'N' are often joined to other letters to form nasalised blends. The initial 'm' or 'n' should not be pronounced as a separate syllable.

Mbuzi	Goat
Mfumu	Chief
Mphatso	Gift

Mvuu	Hippo
Ndodo	Stick, rod
Ngolo	Animal drawn cart
Njerwa	Brick
Nthiti	Rib

Syllabic 'M'

'M' can form a separate syllable when it occurs at the beginning of nouns in the 'Mu-A' and 'Mu-Mi' classes and as the prefix m'- (in).

Mdima	Darkness
Mlomo	Lip
Mnansi	Neighbor
Mtima	Heart
Mzimu	Spirit
M'madzi	In the water
M'mamaŵa	In the morning

Ng'

Ng' is a single nasal sound with no audible 'g' sound. It is pronounced like 'ng' in 'singing'. You may find it hard to pronounce at the beginning of a word because in English this sound never begins a word. Try this progression to train your pronunciation.

1. Say 'singing'.
2. Cut off the 's', say 'inging'.
3. Cut off the 'i', say 'nging'.

Be sure to preserve the sound of the original first 'ng' from 'singing'.

ng'ombe	cow, cattle
ng'oma	drum
sing'anga	native doctor; medicine man (note the first

ng' and second ng are different sounds)

'L' and 'R'

These two letters represent almost the same sound in Chicheŵa, a soft 'l'. In written Chicheŵa there are a set of rules for determining which goes where in a word. To make it brief, 'r' is often written after 'i' or 'e', while 'l' follows 'a', 'o', or 'u'. Only 'l' can begin a word. Note that, because they represent a similar sound, 'l' and 'r' are often mistakenly used interchangeably by many writers.

lero	today
phiri	mountain
phala	porridge
matola	passenger transport

'S' and 'Z' often form blends with other consonants.

dzina	name
tsogolo	future
kupsa	to be ripe or fully cooked

'W' and 'Y' also often form blends with other letters.

bwana	boss
mwayi	chance, opportunity
kudya	to eat
kwambiri	much, very (adverb)

'Ŵ'

'Ŵ' has been an important sound in the typical dialect of Chicheŵa. It seems a growing number of people are replacing it with ordinary 'w'. Much written Chicheŵa ignores it.

It is pronounced by almost saying a 'b' but pushing the air through a small space between the lips rather than actually closing them in the case of a 'b'. The sound is like a very soft 'b'. Be careful not to involve your teeth as you would in pronouncing 'v'.

If you find this letter difficult, you can join those who use an ordinary 'w' in its place. But it is good to be aware of 'ŵ' since it is still widely used.

Malaŵi
Chicheŵa
mawa   tomorrow
nthaŵi   time
kudziŵa   to know

Chapter 2: Tones[1]

Chicheŵa is a 'tonal' language. Part of the meaning of words is conveyed by a higher or lower tone on a word, syllable, or sentence portion.

When we say that a syllable in Chicheŵa has a 'tone', it means that your voice goes up at that point, much the way that it does in English. When a Chicheŵa-speaker says the words 'Maláwi' or 'Kamuzu Bánda', it sounds much the same as an English-speaker saying the same words.

But there are differences from English too. One difference is that in English, an accented syllable can sometimes be pronounced on a low note, for example if the word isn't emphasised or if we ask a question such as 'Malaŵi?' (with -la- on a low note). This doesn't happen in Chicheŵa. The syllable with the tone is always high, even in a question or when it isn't emphasised.

Another difference with English is that there are quite a lot of words in Chicheŵa that have no tone at all. In these words all the syllables are pronounced on a low note. For example, Lilongwe, Kamuzu, nyama 'animal', moŵa 'beer', msika 'market', mtengo 'price', bwino 'well or good'. Now here's the hard part. These words are always pronounced on a low note even when emphasised. So if someone asks Muli bwánji? 'how are you?' you reply 'Ndili bwino' 'I'm fine' with bwino on a low note, even though you might feel like emphasising it. Sometimes adding a tone even changes the meaning. For example, if you add a tone to mtengo 'price' it changes into mténgo 'tree'!

Listen carefully to where your teacher puts the tone.

---

1   Special thanks to Andrew Goodson of Kamuzu Academy for kindly contributing the material of this chapter. I have presented it here almost unchanged.

12

For example, 'thanks!' is 'zíkomo', with the tone on zi-. Don't say zikómo, because it would sound wrong.

When a word has a tone on the last syllable, as in the words nyumbá 'house', Zombá, Chicheŵá, galú 'dog', it can be hard to pronounce. For one thing, the tone in such words tends to spread backwards over both the last two syllables of the word, so that we say not Chicheŵá but Chichéŵá. Sometimes the end part of the tone disappears altogether, leaving just a rising tone on the penultimate syllable: Chichéŵa.

Another thing you will notice about a tone on the final syllable is that it isn't very high. If you ask your teacher to say the two words khúngu 'blindness' and khungú 'skin', you will hear that the second one is pronounced lower than the first, but still not quite as low as a word with no tone like bwino.

Among commonly used words, the word á (wá, chá etc.) 'of' has a tone, so we say á mbúzi 'of a goat' (unlike the toneless a- of the plural such as in agalú 'dogs'). You will hear this tone easily if it is followed by a toneless word, as when you say chábwino 'OK' (literally, 'something of good'). It also has a tone in ápólísi 'policemen', because that means '(men) of the police'.

The word ndí 'and, with' has a tone: ndí mbúzi 'with a goat, and a goat'. But when ndi is a verb meaning 'it is', there is no tone: ndi mbúzi 'it's a goat'. Sí, on the other hand, meaning 'it isn't', does have a tone: sí mbúzi 'it isn't a goat'.

When it comes to verbs, the tones can be rather complicated, but there are certain common patterns which are easy to learn. For example, in the present tense with -ku-, the tone always falls on the syllable following -ku-: ndikupíta 'I'm going', ndikuthándiza 'I'm helping'. The same goes for the infinitive: kuthándiza 'to help'. In the past tense the tone falls on -na-: ndinápita 'I went', ndináthandiza 'I helped'. Some people say ndináthándiza with two tones.

Another common pattern has two separate tones, one on the first syllable (or the first two syllables) and another on the penultimate syllable. This pattern is often found with negative verbs, e.g. síndínapíte 'I didn't go', ósapíta! 'don't go!'. It is also found in the present habitual tense with -ma-, e.g. ndímapíta 'I usually go'.

Commands usually have no tone: pitani! 'go!'. There are a few exceptional verbs, however, in which the command does have a tone, e.g. tsaláni! 'stay!' When a command has a pronoun like ndi- 'me' added to it, you put a tone after the ndi-: ndipátseni! or mundipátse! 'give me!'. In longer verbs there is also a tone on the -e at the end: ndithándízéni! 'help me!'

When it comes to relative tenses, the tones change. The main thing to note is that there is an extra tone on the first syllable. For example, ákúpíta 'while going', and átápíta 'after going'. This also applies to verbs in relative clauses.

When you get good at Chicheŵa you will notice that changing the tones on the verbs sometimes changes the meaning in a subtle way. For example:
síndínapíte 'I didn't help' but sindinapíte 'I haven't helped yet';
síndípita 'I don't go' but sindipíta 'I won't go';
ndinápita 'I went' but ndinapíta 'I went just now (but I came back)';
ndímathandíza 'I usually help' but ndimathándiza 'I was helping';
ndikupíta 'I am going' but ndíkúpíta 'while I was going';
ali 'he is' but áli 'when he is'.

14

However, these are subtleties for advanced learners. The best way to begin is to memorise the patterns of the words and tenses you use most often and gradually build up from there.

In this book, I will not normally mark tones, as they are not generally marked in written Chicheŵa. But I will mention and mark important tone patterns in specific cases in the chapters where they occur.

Chapter 3: Greetings

The formalities of greeting and farewell are a very important part of African communication, and they can be quite different from what you might be used to from your social background. Don't be surprised if you don't find exact correspondents to such common English greetings as: Hi, Hello, Goodbye.

Some books introduce 'Hello' or 'Hi' as 'Moni!' But that is a somewhat uncommon, and, therefore unimportant greeting, especially for the beginner, and has nothing near the usage that 'Hi' and 'Hello' have in English. Instead of a single word for 'Hello', Chicheŵa speakers will generally greet one another with such questions as 'How are you?', 'How did you wake up?', and the like. 'Goodbye' is replaced by such farewells as 'We'll see each other', 'Travel well', and 'Stay well.'

Remember you're not just learning a new language, but also a new way of interacting with people—a new culture. That involves a new set of important greetings. Instead of 'Good morning,' we say 'How did you sleep?' or 'How did you wake up?' And after inquiring after someone's health, one might well go on to ask about family, and if he has time, even to ask about their job, where they were going on Tuesday when they saw them on the road, and how they traveled where they went!

To introduce the most common, basic greetings, I will take you through two different situations: you visiting someone else and you meeting someone on the street.

1. Your visit to someone's house.

You walk up to Jimu's house and you say:
Odi! Odi!   (In lieu of knocking.)
Jimu: Eee!   Yes. (He opens the door.)
        Loŵani.   Come in.

After you are seated:
Jimu: Muli bwanji?   How are you?
                      (The host initiates the greetings.)
You: Ndili bwino. Kaya inu? I am fine. What about you?
Jimu: Ndili bwino.   I am fine.

Instead of the 'Muli bwanji?' greeting, there could be these two variations:

Morning:
Jimu: Mwadzuka bwanji? How did you wake up?
You: Ndadzuka bwino. Kaya inu. I woke up well. What about you?
Jimu: Ndadzuka bwino. I woke up well.

Afternoon:
Jimu: Mwaswera bwanji? How have you spent the day?
You: Ndaswera bwino. Kaya inu? I have spent the day well. What about you?
Jimu: Ndaswera bwino. I have spent it well.

At the end of the visit:
You: Basi, ndapita. That's all. I have gone.
Jimu: Zikomo. Yendani bwino. Thanks. Travel well.
You: Zikomo. Tsalani bwino. Thanks. Stay well.

2. You meeting someone on the street:

You: Muli bwanji, Jimu? How are you, Jim?
Jimu: Ndili bwino, kaya inu? I am fine, how about you?
You: Ndili bwino. I am fine.

Again, there could be the two variations I mentioned in the last example.

After chatting a little:
You: Basi, tionana. That's all. We'll see each other (later).
Jimu: Zikomo. Tionana. Thanks. We'll see each other.
You: Zikomo.   Thanks.

Both you and Jimu could also say 'Yendani bwino,' ('Travel well') to each other instead of 'Tionana.'

18

Chapter 4: Personal Pronouns

I will introduce you to pronouns as a kind of indirect way to get into the verb system, and then from there into the more complex noun system.

1. I = Ine/Ndi-

The English pronoun 'I' is translated 'ine' ('ine' is pronounced 'ee-nay'.)   That is the 'stand-alone' form. It is the single word form. Use it when you want to say 'I' or 'me' without a sentence or for emphasis in the sentence. To use 'I' with a verb in a sentence, we can't use this 'ine' form alone, we must rather use a different form that glues itself on the front of the verb. This form is 'ndi-'. The hyphen at the end shows that it connects on the front of a verb stem. So if you want to say, 'I am going,' you use:
Ine ndikupita. I am going.
Ine/Ndi- = I
Kupita = to go
(The stem here is -pita, ku- is a prefix that indicates 'to' when the verb stands alone, as in 'to go'; it also stays with the verb in the present tense of the verb.)

On most sentences, you can leave off the separate 'Ine' except where you want to give emphasis, because the 'ndi-' on the front of the verb is enough to show that it is 'I' who is doing the action.

Ndikupita. I am going. Ine ndikupita. [As for me,] I am going.

Kubwera. To come. Ndikubwera. I am coming.
Ine ndikubwera. As for me, I am coming.
Kudziŵa. To know. Ndikudziŵa. I know.
Kufika. To arrive. Ndikufika. I am arriving.
Ndili bwino. I am fine.
Ine ndili bwino. As for me, I am fine.

2. We = Ife/Ti-

The word 'we' is 'ife'. Now, just like 'ine,' this 'ife'
is the stand-alone form; so we can't use this form alone with
a verb. Rather we use a different form that connects to the
front of the verb. That form is 'ti-'. So if we want to say,
'We are going,' we won't use 'ife' alone but 'ti-' in front of
the verb stem.

Ife/Ti- = We
We are going.   Tikupita.

Now we can still use the stand-alone form of the
pronoun ('ife') in this sentence but only along with the prefix
form on the verb, like this:

Ife tikupita. [As for us,] we are going.

Kubwera. To come. Tikubwera. We are coming.
Kudziŵa. To know. Tikudziŵa. We know.
Kufika. To arrive. Tikufika. We are arriving.
Tili bwino. We are fine.
Ife tili bwino. As for us, we are fine.

3. You = Inu/Mu-

The word 'you' is 'inu'. The verb prefix form is 'mu-'.

Inu/Mu- = You
You are going. Mukupita.
Inu mukupita. [As for you,] you are going.

Kubwera. To come. Mukubwera. You are coming.
Kudziŵa. To know. Mukudziŵa. You know.
Kufika. To arrive. Mukufika. You are arriving.
Muli bwino. You are fine.
Inu muli bwino. As for you, you are fine.

There's something special you'll want to note about this word 'you' that you've learned:

Inu/Mu- is the plural form for 'you'.

In other words, it really means 'you all' or 'you people'. But it's almost always used even when a single individual is being addressed because it's considered more respectful. So, for respect, always use this form of 'you.'

This next section is on the singular form for 'you'. I have put the sections out of order like this (first plural, then singular) just to call your attention to the fact that the plural form is more common, more important, and more respectful.

4. You (singular) = Iwe/U-

Here's the word 'you' (singular): 'iwe'. The form that

goes on the verb is 'u-'.

Iwe/U- = You (Singular, disrespectful)
You are going.   Ukupita.

Just like other pronouns, if you want you can use both forms together, just be sure to put 'u-' on the verb.

Iwe ukupita. As for you, you are going.

Kubwera. To come. Ukubwera. You are coming.
Kudziŵa. To know. Ukudziŵa. You know.
Kufika. To arrive. Ukufika. You are arriving.
Uli bwanji? How are you?
Iwe uli bwanji? How are you?
Uli bwino. You are fine.
Iwe uli bwino. As for you, you are fine.

Note on usage of Iwe/U-:
Iwe/U- is singular and sometimes disrespectful.

It is appropriately used between friends or when an older person addresses a child. It's not in itself a disrespectful word as such, but rather a very *familiar* word.   So it's very suitable and can even be a term of endearment if one uses it when speaking to close friends or relatives. It is generally not suitable for using with strangers except if the stranger is a young child. Note that even with children you can use the plural, respectful form at any time.   So, get in the habit of using the plural 'you' for everyone. When you have gotten a 'feel' for using this singular form 'iwe'/u- by listening to how people use it, you can also start using it—carefully!

5. He (or she) = Iye/A-

The word 'he/she' is 'iye'. With a verb, 'iye' takes the form 'a-'.

Iye/A- = He (or She)
He/She is going. Akupita.
Iye akupita. He/she is going.

Kubwera. To come. Akubwera. He is coming.
Kudziŵa. To know. Akudziŵa. He knows.
Kufika. To arrive. Akufika. He is arriving.
Ali bwanji? How is he?
Iye ali bwanji? How is he? (a little more emphatic)
Ali bwino. He is fine.
Iye ali bwino. As for him, he is fine.

6. They = Iwo/A-

The word 'they' is 'iwo'. This word 'iwo' changes to 'a-' in front of a verb.

Note: Just like how 'inu' (plural 'you') is more respecfully used of a single person than 'iwe' (singular 'you'), so 'iwo' is sometimes used of a single person to indicate respect! When you are talking about someone to be respected, like a chief or grandmother, you would not talk about 'iye' ('him/her') but 'iwo' ('they').

Notice that the form that goes before a verb ('a-') is the same as the form for 'iye' ('he/she'). Don't let that bother you. Usually the context will help you know which is which.

Iwo/A- = They
They are going. Akupita.
Iwo akupita. [As for them,] they are going.

Kubwera. To come. Akubwera. They are coming.
Kudziŵa. To know. Akudziŵa. They know.
Kufika. To arrive. Akufika. They are arriving.
Ali bwino. They are fine.
Iwo ali bwino. As for them, they are fine.

Summary:

You have now learned the personal pronouns used as doers of action in a sentence. In order, they are:

Ine	I	Ife	we
Iwe	you (singular)	Inu	you (plural)
Iye	he/she	Iwo	they

These are the forms that go in front of verbs:

Ndi-	I	Ti-	we
U-	you (singular)	Mu-	you (plural)
A-	he, she	A-	they

Remember: to use a pronoun as a subject of a sentence (as in 'he is going') the pronoun can be merely a prefix on the front of the verb, or both the prefix form and the whole word form can be used together.

When the stand-alone pronoun is used along with the prefix form in front of a verb it's sometimes more emphatic, although not always.

Ine ndikupita. *I am going, not you, not him. I am going; but I don't know what* you *will be doing. Or, simply: I am going.*

Also remember: 'Inu' and 'Iwo' are plural forms that can be used to refer to single individuals for respect. In fact, 'inu' is the ordinary 'you' word that should be used almost all the time!

Chapter 5: Object Pronouns

So far we've just looked at pronouns that act as doers of the action. '<u>He</u> is going.' '<u>I</u> am eating.' When a pronoun is used as a receiver of action (object), its usage is a little different and sometimes the form is different as well. What is the difference between the words 'he' and 'him'? The meaning is just the same, but when one is used 'he' does action and when the other is used action is done to 'him.'

'The monster eats him.' vs. 'He eats the monster.'

Not: 'The monster eats he.' or 'Him eats the monster.'

Object pronouns (pronouns that have action done to them) take:

a. A form that goes on the verb: Aku-<u>ndi</u>-dziŵa. He knows me. (The form that goes on the verb always is in the position you see it here, right in front of the verb stem, which in this case is -dziŵa.)

b. Or both a form that goes on the verb and a stand-alone form: Aku-<u>ndi</u>-dziŵa <u>ine</u>. He knows me.

The object infix takes a high tone: *Akundídzíŵa*. Note that the tense we are using here also puts a high tone on the first syllable of the verb stem, thus the second high tone mark in '*Akundídzíŵa*.' Tones are not normally marked in writing, but remember that the object infix takes a high tone.

Let's go through all six of the personal pronouns one by one to see how their object forms work:

1. Me = Ine/-ndi-
As in 'Akundídzíŵa ine.' 'He knows me.'

He knows.   Akudziŵa.
He knows me. Akundidziŵa. -or- Iye akundidziŵa ine.
-or- Iye akundidziŵa. -or- Akundidziŵa ine. (The basic meaning of all of these sentences is the same, but there are slight differences of emphasis that should be obvious.)

To see. Kuona.   To see me. Kundiona ine.
You see. Mukuona.   You see me. Mukundiona ine.
They see. Akuona.   They see me. Akundiona ine. (You would add 'iwo' at the front to make it ultra clear that you are referring to 'them', instead of 'he/she', as the ones who 'saw me', since the 'a-' prefix can be ambiguous there.)
She sees. Akuona.   She sees me. Akundiona ine.

To want. Kufuna.   To want me. Kundifuna. -or-
Kundifuna ine.
John wants me. John akundifuna.   John akundifuna ine. Iye akundifuna.   Akundifuna ine.

To hear. Kumva.
To hear me. Kundimva. -or- Kundimva ine.
Thoko and Gire are hearing me.   Thoko ndi Gire akundimva. Thoko ndi Gire akundimva ine. Iwo akundimva. Akundimva. Iwo akundimva ine.

2. Us = Ife/-ti-
As in 'Akutídzíŵa ife.' 'He knows us.'
Remember to pronounce a high tone on the -ti-, as with all the object infixes.

Kuona. To see. Kutiona. To see us. Kutiona ife. To see us.
Iwe ukutiona. You (singular) see us.

27

Ukutiona. Ukutiona ife. Iwe ukuona ife.
Inu mukutiona. You (plural) see us.
Mukutiona ife. Inu mukutiona ife.
Yobu akutiona. Job sees us. Iye akutiona ife. Akutiona.

Kufuna. To want.
Kutifuna. To want us. Kutifuna ife. To want us.
Amfumu akutifuna. The chief (respectful plural) wants us.
Iwo akutifuna. He (literally: 'they') wants us.
Akutifuna ife. Akutifuna.
She wants us. Iye akutifuna. Akutifuna ife.

3. You (singular) = Iwe/-ku-
As in 'Akukúdzíŵa iwe.' 'He knows you (singular).'

Now this pronoun takes an unexpected form for the part that
goes in the verb: '-ku-'!

Kuona. To see. Kukuona. To see you (singular)/seeing you.
Akuona. He sees.
Akukuona. He sees you. Iye akukuona iwe. He sees you.

Kufuna. To want.
Kukufuna iwe. To want you. (singular)/wanting you.
Thokozire akukufuna. Thokozire wants you.
Thokozire akukufuna iwe. Thokozire wants you.

Kumva. To hear.
Kukumva iwe. To hear you (singular)/hearing you.
Akukumva. They are hearing you.
Iwo akukumva iwe. They are hearing you.

28

4. You (plural) = Inu/-ku- -ni

As in 'Akukúdzíŵani inu.' 'He knows you (plural).'

The form of this pronoun that sticks in the verb is almost the same as the last one but just with the addition of the '-ni' on the end of the verb.

Kuona. To see. Kukuonani. To see you (plural)/seeing you.
Kukuonani inu. To see you/seeing you (plural).
Ana akukuonani. The children see you.
Tikukuonani. We see you. Tikukuonani ife. We see you.
(Notice that the 'ife' seems to be in the 'wrong' place, but this merely changes the emphasis of the sentence.)

Kufuna. To want. Ndikukufunani. I want you.
Ine ndikukufunani inu. I want you. Inu ndikukufunani.
(Placing the 'inu' first can change the emphasis.)

Kumva. To hear. Kukumvani. To hear you/hearing you.
Kukumvani inu. To hear you/hearing you.
Ife tikukumvani inu. We are hearing you.

5. Him or her = Iye/-mu-

As in 'Akumúdzíŵa iye.' 'He knows him/her.'

Don't be confused by the similarity of this -mu- and the mu- that refers to 'inu' as the 'doer' of an action. Look at this sentence:

Mu-ku-mú-dzíŵa.

The first 'mu' is before the 'ku' so it is a 'doer' of the

29

action. 'Mu' as a doer of the action always refers to 'inu' which is 'you' (plural). The second 'mu' is after the 'ku' and thus must be a receiver of the action. 'Mu' as a receiver of action always refers to 'iye' and thus means 'he' or 'she'.

Here let me give you an important rule:
The order of prefixes and infixes on the verb itself is fixed. Subject prefixes have a special slot, object infixes have a special slot, and tense markers (like '-ku-' which I haven't yet discussed) have their special slot, so if it seems like a certain particle is in what looks like a 'wrong' slot, it means it probably has a different meaning than when it was in the slot you thought it was supposed to go in.

Kuthandiza. To help/helping.
Kumuthandiza. Helping him/her.
Kumuthandiza iye. Helping him/her.
Mukuthandiza John. You are helping John.
Mukumuthandiza. You are helping him.
John mukumuthandiza. You are helping John.
John mukumuthandiza inu. You are helping John.

Kuphunzitsa. To teach.
Kumuphunzitsa. To teach him/her, teaching him/her.
I am teaching the child. Ndikumuphunzitsa mwana.
I am teaching him. Iye ndikumuphunzitsa.

Kusoŵa. To lack, be missing, miss, need, be needed.
John akusoŵa. John is missing.
Ine ndikumusoŵa John. I miss/need John.
Iwe ukusoŵa. You (singular) are missing.
(We haven't seen you lately.)

Iwe ukumusoŵa. You (singular) miss him/her.
(See how the meaning of this verb {'kusoŵa'} changes from 'be missing' to 'miss' by putting an object/receiver of the action with it.)

6. Them = Iwo/-ŵa-
As in 'Ndikuŵádzíŵa iwo.' 'I know them.'

Kuthandiza. To help. Kuŵathandiza. To help them.
Iye akuŵathandiza. He is helping them.
Akuŵathandiza iwo. He/she/they are helping them.
Ndikuŵathandiza ine. I am helping them.
Inu mukuŵathandiza. You are helping them.
Tikuŵathandiza John ndi Thoko. We are helping John and Thoko.
Tikuthandiza John ndi Thoko. We are helping John and Thoko.
Ife tikuŵathandiza. We are helping them.

Kugwira. To catch, hold onto, grab, touch, etc.
Kugwira iwo. Grabbing them/To grab them.
Kuŵagwira. Grabbing them/ To grab them.
Wapolisi akugwira anthu. The policeman is catching people.
Iye akuŵagwira. He is catching them.

Kusoŵa. To need, be needed, lack, be lacked, be missed, miss.
Iwo akusoŵa. They are missing/haven't been seen for some time.
Iye akuŵasoŵa. He/she misses them. Iye akuŵasoŵa iwo. He/she misses them.

Ine ndikuŵasoŵa. I miss them.
Iwo ndikuŵasoŵa. I miss them.
Iwo tikuŵasoŵa. We miss them.
Ndikuŵasoŵa iwo. I miss them.
Tikuŵasoŵa iwo. We miss them.

Good Manners:
Remember that 'iwo' is often used for individuals to show
respect. For extra respect:
'Iwo ali bwanji?' How are they?
'Iwo ali bwanji?' How is he/she?
('Iye ali bwanji?' is less respectful.)
'Iwo ali bwanji?' How are you (very respectful)?
Context alone helps you know for sure who is being talked
about or to.

Pronoun Summary:
All the stand-alone personal pronouns are:

Ine	I	Ife	we
Iwe	you (singular)	Inu	you
Iye	he/she	Iwo	they

The prefixes used when the pronoun is the subject:

Ndi-	I	Ti-	we
U-	you (singular)	Mu-	you (plural, respect)
A-	he, she	A-	they

As in:
Kuvuta   To cause trouble…
(Ine) Ndikuvuta   (Ife) Tikuvuta

(Iwe) Ukuvuta

(Inu) Mukuvuta

(Iye) Akuvuta

(Iwo) Akuvuta

Infixes used when the pronoun is the object (as acted upon):

-ndi-	I	-ti-		we
-ku-	you (singular)	-ku-	-ni	you (plural, respect)
-mu-	he, she	-ŵa-		they

As in:

Kuvuta   To cause trouble to…

Iye akuvúta.   He/She is causing trouble.

Akundívúta	(ine)	Akutívúta	(ife)
Akukúvúta	(iwe)	Akukúvútani	(inu)
Akumúvúta	(iye)	Akuŵávúta	(iwo)

I have marked the tones here as a reminder.

Chapter 6: The Perfect Tense

Up to this point we've just been using one verb tense (time perspective) for all our practice sentences. That tense is what might be called present tense, or present continuous tense.

Ndikupita. I am going.

Ndikudziŵa. I know.

Akufuna. He wants.

Akusoŵa. They are missing.

There's another tense I would like us to look at before we jump into anything else. This tense is what can be called the **perfect tense**.

For the first tense we learned, the tense marker, or the sign that showed what tense we were in was '-ku-', followed by a high tone syllable. 'Ndikupíta.' But in the perfect tense the marker is '-a-', characterized by a low tone on the whole verb. Now this '-a-' goes in the same place as the '-ku-' went in the verb. So look at this example:

Inu mukupita. You are going. (Present Continuous Tense)

Inu mu-a-pita. You have gone. (Perfect Tense)

But really it always gets shortened to:

Inu mwapita. You have gone.

1. Perfect tense with I = (Ndi-a-) = Nda-

Kupita. To go/going. Ndapita. I have gone.

Ine ndapita. Ndapita ine. I have gone.

('Ndapita,' 'I have left,' is a common way to tell your host that you are now leaving, even though you haven't really left yet!)

2. Perfect tense with We = (Ti-a-) = Ta-

Kuthandiza. To help/helping. Tathandiza. We have helped.
Ife tathandiza. Tathandiza ife.

Note: the object pronoun infix still carries the high tone in
perfect tense verbs. I have marked them here only.

Takúthandiza. We have helped you (singular).
Takúthandizani. We have helped you (plural). Or: Ife
takúthandizani. Ife takúthandizani inu. Takúthandizani inu.
Tamúthandiza. We have helped him/her.
Tawâthandiza. We have helped them.

3. Perfect tense with You (singular) = (U-a-) = Wa-

Kuona. To see. Waona. You (singular) have seen (lately).
Iwe waona. Waona iwe.

Wandiona. You (singular) have seen me.
Wationa. You (singular) have seen us.
Wamuona. You (singular) have seen him/her. Or: Iwe
wamuona. Wamuona iwe. Iwe wamuona iye.
Wawâona. You (singular) have seen them.

4. Perfect tense with You (plural/respectful) = (Mu-a-) = Mwa-

Kugwira. To catch, grab, hold, touch, etc. Mwagwira. You
have caught, etc.

Mwandigwira.   You (plural) have caught me.
Mwatigwira. You (plural) have held onto us.
Mwamugwira. You (plural) have touched him/her.
Mwaŵagwira. You (plural) have grabbed them. Or: Inu
mwaŵagwira. Iwo mwaŵagwira. Inu mwaŵagwira iwo.
Iwo mwaŵagwira inu.

5. Perfect tense with He/she = Wa-

That's right! This one seems like an exception. For present
tense, 'he' is 'a-', but for perfect tense, instead of saying
'a-a-' we say 'u-a-'='wa-'. So our perfect tense prefix for
'iye' is 'wa-', which is the same as the one for 'iwe' (you
singular). The context usually makes it clear as to which
one is being meant.

Kumva. To hear. Wamva. He/she has heard. Wamva iye.
Iye wamva.

Wandimva. He/she has heard me.
Or: Iye wandimva.   Iye wandimva ine. Wandimva ine.
Watimva.   He/she has heard us.
Wakumva. He/she has heard you (singular).
Wakumvani. He/she has heard you (plural).
Wamumva.   He/she has heard him/her.
Waŵamva. He/she has heard them.

6. Perfect tense with They = (A-a) = A-

Kuchoka. To leave, go away.
Achoka. They have left. Iwo achoka. Achoka iwo.
Kulira. To cry. Alira. They have cried. Iwo alira. Alira iwo.

36

Summary of Perfect Tense Personal Pronouns:

Here are all the personal pronouns as they are used in the perfect tense.

I have gone.	Ine ndapita.
We have gone.	Ife tapita.
You (s) have gone.	Iwe wapita.
You (pl) have gone.	Inu mwapita.
He/she have gone.	Iye wapita.
They have gone.	Iwo apita.

Use of the Perfect Tense

This tense is used to show that action has occurred and has continuing impact on the present. Of course, this has to do with the context in which one is speaking.

Ndagula nyumba. I have bought a house (and still own it). (kugula – to buy)
Ndapeza chakudya. I have found food (and am now eating it). (kupeza – to find; chakudya – food)
Mwakwatira. You have gotten married (and still are married). (kukwatira – to marry)

Some of the greetings you learned use this perfect tense:
'Mwadzuka bwanji?' 'Ndadzuka bwino.' ('How have you woken up?' 'I have woken up well.')
'Mwaswera bwanji?' 'Ndaswera bwino.' ('How have you spent the day?' 'I have spent the day well.')

This tense will not always be translated into English with

the English perfect tense.

After being swindled of his money, one might say to the swindler: 'Ndakudziŵa!' translated as, 'I know you (now)!'

Chapter 7: Past Tense and Future Tense

The two tenses learned so far have been present tense and perfect tense.

The present tense marker is '-ku-', followed by a high tone:
Akupíta. Ndikufúna. Mukusówa.

The perfect tense marker is '-a-', low tone:
Mwapita. Ndafuna. Asoŵa.

Now let's look at two more tenses: past tense and future tense.

Past Tense is shown by the marker '-ná-' or '-dá-'.

The '-ná-' form seems to have more widespread usage, but '-dá-' is still to be encountered. Note that there is a high tone on the -ná- and -dá-. I have marked them in this chapter, but the tones are not usually marked in writing.

Look at these sentences.

Ndinápita.	I went.
Tinápita.	We went.
Unápita.	You (singular) went.
Munápita.	You (plural) went.
Anápita.	He/she went.
Anápita.	They went.

Ine ndináfuna.	I wanted.
Ife tináfuna.	We wanted.
Iwe unáfuna.	You (s) wanted.
Inu munáfuna.	You (pl) wanted.

Iye anáfuna.	He/she wanted.
Iwo anáfuna.	They wanted.

Pronoun	Present Tense	Perfect Tense	Past Tense
Ine	Ndikupíta	Ndapita	Ndinápita
Ife	Tikupíta	Tapita	Tinápita
Iwe	Ukupíta	Wapita	Unápita
Inu	Mukupíta	Mwapita	Munápita
Iye	Akupíta	Wapita	Anápita
Iwo	Akupíta	Apita	Anápita

Future Tense is shown by the marker 'dzá'.
Note the high tone, -dzá-.

Ine ndidzásoŵa.	I will be missing/not available.
Ife tidzásoŵa.	We will be missing/not available.
Iwe udzásoŵa.	You (s) will be missing/not available.
Inu mudzásoŵa.	You (pl) will be missing/not available.
Iye adzásoŵa.	He/she will be missing/not available.
Iwo adzásoŵa.	They will be missing/not available.

Ndidzádzuka.	I will wake up.
Tidzádzuka.	We will wake up.
Udzádzuka.	You (s) will wake up.
Mudzádzuka.	You (pl) will wake up.
Adzádzuka.	He/she will wake up.
Adzádzuka.	They will wake up.

Past Tense Usage:

The past tense that we have learned above, which is indicated by the -ná- marker, can be used for many statements referring to simple completed past action.

Ndinápita ku Lilongwe.	I went to Lilongwe.

40

Anáfuna kupita.	He/she wanted to go.
Anándídziŵa ine.	He knew me.
Anáwádziŵa.	He knew them.
Ine ndináwámva iwo.	I heard them.
Ndinámúona iye.	I saw him.
Munámúdziŵa.	You knew her.
Munátíthandiza ife.	You helped us.
Unáona mayi.	You (singular, familiar) saw mother.
Anáfuna kupita.	They wanted to go.
Iwo anándíona ine.	They saw me.
Tinákúonani inu.	We saw you.

Future Tense Usage:

This future tense indicated by -dzá- refers to events that will take place in the general or more distant future (that is, not today). There is another future tense to be studied in a later chapter that looks more at close events, events that are right about to happen.

Ndidzákúfuna iwe.	I will want/need you.
Iye adzátímva ife.	He will hear us.
Pule adzámúona.	Pule will see him/her.

tsopano	now
m'mamaŵa	in the morning
dzulo	yesterday
maŵa	tomorrow

Mwandida akubwéra tsopano.   Mwandida is coming

now.

Mwandida wabwera m'mamaŵa.   Mwandida came in the morning (and is still here).

Mwandida anábwera dzulo.   Mwandida came yesterday.

Mwandida adzábwera maŵa. Mwandida will come tomorrow.

Ndikufúna kukúdziŵani.   I want to know you.

Ndafuna kukúdziŵani.   I have been wanting to know you.

Ndináfuna kukúdziŵani.   I wanted to know you (at a certain point in the past).

Ndidzáfuna kukúdziŵani.   I will want to know you.

42

Chapter 8: Introduction to Nouns

While we were going through pronouns, you were introduced to the fact that verbs always take a prefix to point back to the subject (the doer of the action).

For example, you can't just say, 'Ine kupita,' to say, 'I am going.' You have to say, 'Ine ndikupita,' or even, 'Ndikupita.' So, the prefix form of the pronoun is more important than the 'stand-alone' form of the pronoun. This is also true for nouns (words for things or people). In order to say, 'The thing is going,' we put together the words 'chinthu' (thing) and 'kupita' (to go), by adding a prefix 'chi-' on the front of the verb.

Chinthu chikupita.   The thing is going.

Now, just like with pronouns, the 'chi-' will always stay. If you have already said 'chinthu' in another sentence, you can leave it out of this one, and just say, 'Chikupita.' Here the 'chi-' stands for 'it'. So: 'It is going.' This is just like with pronouns, where 'Ndikupita,' means 'I am going,' just as much as, 'Ine ndikupita.'

In Chicheŵa, nouns are arranged into several classes, every class having its own way of showing plural and its own special prefixes to go on verbs and adjectives. For example, all the nouns in the class with the unfortunate name 'Chi-zi' (pronounced like 'cheesy!') start with 'chi-' and connect to verbs by adding 'chi-' to the verb. 'Chinthu' is an example of a word in this 'chi-zi' class. So that's why, when we used 'chinthu' with the verb 'kupita', 'to go,' we said, 'Chinthu chikupita.'

Words in the same class with 'chinthu' show plural by changing that 'chi-' in front of the word to 'zi-.'

chinthu\zinthu – thing\things

This change in the word itself causes a corresponding change in the prefix that goes on the verb. Where we had, 'Chinthu chikupita,' before, now we have, 'Zinthu zikupita.' Notice that the 'zi-' on the verb corresponds to the 'zi-' on the noun.

That's just one class of nouns! Each class of nouns will have a unique way of forming plural and relating to verbs and adjectives. The general rules you should pick up are:
1. Plural is usually shown by a change on the first syllable of the noun.
2. A noun shows agreement with a verb or adjective in the sentence by a prefix on the verb or adjective.

The noun system might appear rather complex at first, but it follows certain rules closely and exceptions are few and easily learned. It will take a little rote memorization, but if you have enough exposure and practice with the real thing you'll pick it up quickly. Try to figure out the patterns and general rules that emerge, and that will really help you cope with it.

It is helpful to know that the first syllable of each noun is the 'relational' part, showing how the noun forms plural and how it connects with other words in the sentence. For example, we have the word, 'munthu' in which the first syllable is 'mu-.' You will learn that the 'mu-' on this word shows that it is a singular of the 'Mu A' class, forms plural by replacing 'mu-' with 'a-,' and connects with verbs by adding an 'a-' on the front of the verb.   The last '-nthu' never changes.

Rule: *Words that have the same first letters or sounds often (not always) go in the same class: that is they form plural in the same way and connect to verbs and adjectives in the same way.*

According to the listing that I give you here, there are eleven noun classes.   These classes have been given names and numbers to help in organizing and learning them.   You will find that some other listings have the later classes in different orders and that different books often give different names for the same classes.   Some even put the singular and plural forms in their own separate classes, thus almost doubling the number of classes.

	Class Name	Singular Noun	Plural Form	Verb Prefix	Adj. Prefix
1	Mu A	Mu-, M-, Mw-	A-	A-/A-	Wa-/A-
2	Mu Mi	Mu-, M-, Mw-	Mi-	U-/I-	Wa-/Ya-
3	Chi Zi	Chi-	Zi-	Chi-/Zi-	Cha-/Za-
4	I Zi or N	N-, Mph-, Mb-, Mv-, I-	no change	I-/Zi-	Ya-/Za-
5	Li Ma	others (b,d,l, k,g,t,etc.)	add Ma-	Li-/A-	La-/A-
6	U Ma	U-	add Ma-	U-/A-	Wa-/A-

7	Ka Ti	Ka-	Ti-	Ka-/Ti-	Ka-/Ta-
8	Ku Verbal	Ku-	-----	Ku-	Kwa-
9	Ku	Ku-	-----	Ku-	Kwa-
10	Pa	Pa-	-----	Pa-	Pa-
11	Mu	Mu-	-----	Mu-	Mwa-

Note on articles (a, an, the):

Now that we're getting into nouns, I think it's important to mention that there are no articles in Chicheŵa like the English 'a,' 'an' or 'the'.

A word like 'chinthu' could be translated 'a thing,' 'the thing,' or merely 'thing'.

Try to forget about 'a,' 'an' and 'the.' Just imagine they don't exist. Sometimes however, the word 'the' in English actually is used to mean 'that'. In such a case, Chicheŵa would use the word for 'that' that would fit with the noun being used. Otherwise, just ignore 'a,' 'an,' and 'the'!

Chapter 9: The Noun Classes

1 Mu-A Class

The Mu-A class, usually considered the 'first' class, includes most people words (person, teacher, woman, etc.). Many of these start with the letters M-, Mu-, Mw- (munthu – person, mwana – child). It also includes many words that start with other letters as well (bambo – father).

Usually, this class forms plural by replacing the m-, mu-, or mwa- with a- (munthu\anthu – person\people). In the case of words that begin with other letters than 'm-', the a- is just added on the beginning of the original word (bambo\abambo – father\fathers).

Besides people, this class also includes many animal, bird, and tree names (e.g. galu – dog, mphaka – cat), as well as quite a few words that refer to food substances or uncountable things (katundu – luggage, stuff; fodya – tobacco) and some words from English origin (buledi – bread; tiyi – tea).

Besides the ordinary use of the plural, the plural is often used to show respect for the person referred to, just like we saw in connection with plural 'you'. The form for respectful plural is the same as that of numerical plural, the initial 'a-'. ('Zikomo, aphunzitsi.' 'Thank you, teacher.')

Vocabulary:

Singular	Plural	Meaning
-People-		
mkazi	akazi	woman, wife
mwamuna	amuna	man, husband
bambo	abambo	father, man, sir
mayi	amayi	mother, ma'am

mzibambo	azibambo	man (alt. of 'bambo')
mzimayi	azimayi	woman (alt. of 'mayi')
mnyamata	anyamata	young man
mtsikana	atsikana	young woman
mwana	ana	child
m'bale	abale	relative
mzungu	azungu	European
mphunzitsi	aphunzitsi	teacher

-Animals, Birds, Trees-

galu	agalu	dog
mphaka	amphaka	cat
pusi	apusi	cat, monkey
kalulu	akalulu	rabbit
kadzidzi	akadzidzi	owl
kachere	akachere	wild fig

-Food, Uncountable Words-

fodya	-----	tobacco
shuga	-----	sugar
anyezi	-----	onions
tomato	-----	tomato
kachewere	-----	potato
katundu	-----	luggage/stuff

Note: Use the title 'bambo' to refer to any grown man.
'Zikomo, bambo.' Thank you, sir. 'Bambo Phiri' Mr. Phiri.
Use the word, 'mayi,' to refer to any grown woman.
'Zikomo, mayi.' Thank you, ma'am.' 'Mayi Phiri.' Mrs. Phiri.

Subject (doer of action):
To use words in this class with verbs, use 'a-' just as you learned for the personal pronouns 'iye' ('he/she') or 'iwo' ('they' or 'he/she' respectful).

Mwana akupita. The child is going.
Mzungu ali bwino, koma akusoŵa. The white person is fine, but (koma) he is missing/not around.
Mnyamata anachoka. The young man left.
Mtsikana anapita dzulo, wapita lero, ndipo adzapita maŵa. The young woman went yesterday, has gone today, and will go tomorrow. (ndipo – and, joining clauses)
Anyamata ndi atsikana adzabwera maŵa. Boys and girls will come tomorrow. (ndi – and, joining words or phrases)

Object (receiver of action):
When a word in the 'Mu A Class' is seen as having something done to it, when it is the object of the verb, it acts just like the pronouns for 'he/she' and 'they' (iye and iwo).
That is, we can say:
Ndikufuna mwana. I want the child.
As well as,
Ndikumufuna mwana. I want the child.
Just like,
Ndikumufuna iye. I want him.

Remember there is always a high tone on the object infix:
Ndikumúfúna tiyi. I want the tea.

To help. Kuthandiza. I am helping the man/husband. Ine ndikumuthandiza mwamuna. or, Ndikuthandiza mwamuna.

Mwamuna ndikumuthandiza ine.

To see. Kuona. You saw the child. Munaona mwana. or, Munamuona mwana. Inu munaona mwana. Munamuona iye.

We are helping the boys. Tikuthandiza anyamata. or, Anyamata tikuŵathandiza. Tikuŵathandiza anyamata. Anyamata tikuŵathandiza ife. Ife tikuŵathandiza iwo.

Kumanga. To tie, tighten.
Munthu anamanga galu. A person tied up the dog.
Munthu anam'manga. Someone tied it up (the dog). (Note that -mu- is usually shortened to -m'- before a consonant.)
Atsikana anam'manga dzulo. The girls tied it up yesterday.

2 Mu-Mi Class

The Mu-Mi Class is made up of many words that start with *syllabic* M, Mu, or Mw that are not found in the Mu-A Class; that is, most words starting with syllabic M that don't refer to people or animals.

Nasal blends Mb, Mf, Mph, Mv, do not have a syllabic M; the M is blended with the consonant next to it. Words starting with such blends are excluded from this class and the Mu-A Class.

Plural in this Mu-Mi Class is indicated by replacing the m- or mu- with mi-.

50

Vocabulary:

Singular	Plural	Meaning
mpando	mipando	chair
mpeni	mipeni	knife
mpingo	mipingo	church
mpunga	----	rice
msika	misika	market
mtengo	mitengo	tree
mudzi	midzi	village
munda	minda	garden
mwezi	miyezi	month, moon
moyo	miyoyo	life

Other vocabulary:

kudula	to cut off, cut down
kukwera	to climb, rise
kutha	to run out, finish
kugwa	to fall
kudya	to eat
kodi	introduces a question

Mu-Mi words as subjects:

When used as a subject of a verb, these nouns put 'u-' on front of the verb for singular and 'i-' for plural.

Remember: Mu-Mi rhymes with u-, i-!

Mtengo ukugwa. Mitengo ikugwa. The tree is falling. The trees are falling.
Mpando unagwa. Mipando inagwa. The chair fell. The chairs fell.
Mwezi ukukwera. The moon is going higher in the sky.

Mpeni watha (Perfect tense: u-a- = wa-, i-a- = ya-.). Mipeni yatha. The knife has worn out. The knives have worn out. Mpunga udzatha. The rice will run out. Mpunga ukutha. The rice is running out.

Mu-Mi words as objects of a verb:

When used as objects of the verb (something is being done to them), Mu-Mi nouns insert -u- for singular and -i- for plural between the tense marker and the verb.

Ndikuúdúla mténgo.   I am cutting the tree.

John will cut down the tree with (ndi) the knife.   Yohane adzadula mtengo ndi mpeni. Adzaudula ndi mpeni. Mtengo adzaudula ndi mpeni. Mtengo adzaudula Yohane.
You (s) are cutting the tree. Iwe ukudula mtengo.
You (s) are cutting it. Ukuudula.
You (s) have cut it. Waudula. Iwe waudula mtengo.
Mtengo waudula iwe. Iwe wadula mtengo.

Kodi mukudya mpunga?	Are you eating rice?
Eee! Ndikuudya.	Yes! I am eating it.
Mpunga watha.	The rice has run out.
Mtengo wagwa.	A tree has fallen.
Anthu anaidula mitengo.	People cut the trees down.

3 Chi-Zi Class

This might be the simplest and easiest-to-remember class. It very simply consists of words beginning with ch-, like chinthu (thing), chingwe (string), and chimfine (head cold).

Plural is formed by replacing the ch- with z-. Examples: chambo\zambo (popular fish), chingwe\zingwe (string, rope), cholinga\zolinga (goal, aim).

Vocabulary:

Singular	Plural	Meaning
chaka	zaka	year
chala	zala	finger, toe
chifukwa	zifukwa	reason, because
chikondi	----	love
chimanga	----	maize
chingwe	zingwe	string, rope
chinthu	zinthu	thing
chipatala	zipatala	hospital, clinic
chitseko	zitseko	door

Other vocabulary:

kuyenda	to move, travel
kupweteka	to hurt, be hurt
kusoŵa	to be missing, lost, to lack something
kuona	to see
kupeza	to find
kugwira	to grab, hold onto

Chi-Zi words as subjects:
After a chi-zi noun, merely put 'chi-' on the verb.
Chinthu chikuyenda. A thing is moving.
For plural, put 'zi-' on the verb.
Zinthu zikuyenda. Things are moving. (Actually a common greeting. 'Things are going [well].')
Chitseko chinagwa. The door fell.
Chala chikupweteka. The finger hurts.

Chingwe chasoŵa. (Perfect tense: cha-\za-) The string is lost.
Zingwe zasoŵa. The strings are lost.
Kutha. To run out, be finished. Chimanga chatha. The maize has run out.
Zipatala zili bwino. Hospitals are good.

Chi-Zi words as objects of the verb:
Just put the -chí- or -zí- infix between the tense marker and the verb.

Chinthu ndináchípeza.   I found it, the thing.
Zinthu ndinázíona.   I saw them, the things.

Remember: the -chi- or -zi- can be left off if the noun is named and the sentence order is normal.

Ine ndikufuna chingwe. I want a string.
Ndikuchifuna. I want it.
Tinachigwira. We grabbed it.
Mudzachiona. You will see it.
Mudzaziona zinthu. You will see the things.

Ndapeza chifukwa. I have found the reason. Ndachipeza chifukwa. Chifukwa ndachipeza. Ndachipeza.
Kodi unapeza chitseko iwe? (Kodi merely indicates that the sentence is a question.) Did you (singular) find a door?
Eee, ndinachipeza. Yes, I found it.

    Here are more sentences including words from Mu-A, Mu-Mi, and Chi-Zi classes, used as both subjects and objects:

54

Munthu akudula mtengo ndi kuuchotsa. (kuchotsa – to remove). A person is cutting a tree and removing it.
Munaudula chifukwa chiyani? Why did you cut it (the tree)? (chifukwa chiyani – why, for what reason)
Ndinaudula chifukwa ndinafuna kuuchotsa. I cut it because I wanted to remove it.
Mnyamata wagwira chingwe. A boy has grabbed a string.
Anachigwira chifukwa chiyani? Why did he grab it?
Anagwira chingwe chifukwa anafuna kuchidula. He grabbed the string because he wanted to cut it.
Chaka chapita. The year has gone by.
Zaka zapita. Years have gone by.
Zaka zinapita. Years went by.
Zaka zidzapita. Years will go by.
Ichi ndi chiyani? What is this? (this – ichi, is – ndi)
Ndi chimanga. It is maize.
Ichi ndi chiyani? What is this?
Ndi mpunga. It is rice.
Mpunga uli bwino. Rice is good.
Mtsikana anadya mpunga. The girl ate rice.
Anaudya chifukwa anaufuna. She ate it because she wanted it.

4 I-Zi Class, N Class

This class consists of words beginning with the following letters and blends: N, Mb, Mf, Mv, Mph, and I.

The I-Zi class is unique in that there is no change in the word itself when it becomes plural.

Vocabulary:

Singular	Plural	Meaning
nthaŵi	nthaŵi	time
nyumba	nyumba	house
nthochi	nthochi	banana
ndalama	ndalama	money
mphepo	mphepo	wind, weather
mvula	mvula	rain
ntchito	ntchito	work
nyama	nyama	meat, edible animal
nsima	nsima	thick, maize porridge staple
ndiwo	ndiwo	relish, eaten with nsima or rice
njala	njala	hunger or famine
njira	njira	way, path, method
nkhuku	nkhuku	chicken

I-Zi words as subjects:

When words from the I-Zi class are used as subjects of verbs (doers of action), they put 'i-' on the verb in singular and 'zi-' on the verb in plural.

Nyumba ikugwa. The house is falling.
Nyumba zikugwa. The houses are falling.
As there is no difference in spelling or pronunciation between the plural and singular forms of 'nyumba,' the only difference lies in whether one puts 'i-' or 'zi-' on the verb.

Nkhuku zikuyenda. The chickens are walking.
Ntchito ikuyenda. The work is going forward.
Mvula ikubwera. The rain is coming.
Nyama zikuyenda. The animals are walking.

I-Zi words as objects (receivers of action):
Insert '-í-' or '-zí-' between the tense marker and the verb.

Akuífúna nyama. He wants the meat.

Kupha. To kill.
Kupha nyama. To kill an animal.
Kuipha. To kill it (nyama). Kuzipha. To kill them (nyama).

Kuphika. To cook.
Kuphika ndiwo. To cook ndiwo.
Kuiphika. To cook it (ndiwo). Kuziphika. To cook them (ndiwo's).

Ichi ndi chiyani? What is this?
Nkhuku. A chicken.
Tikufuna kuiphika ndi kuidya. We want to cook it and eat it.
Nkhuku zili bwino. Chickens are good.
Tidzazidya. We will eat them.

5 Li-Ma Class

This is probably the class including the most variety. It includes all Chicheŵa words not included in the Mu-A class and not starting with M, N, Ch, or a vowel.

Mu-A Class contains primarily people, animal, bird, and tree names, some of which start with m-, mu-, or mw-.
Mu-Mi Class contains other words beginning with syllabic m-, mu-, and mw-.
Chi-Zi Class contains all words starting with ch-.
I-Zi Class contains almost all words starting with N-,

nonsyllabic M-'s, and I-.

What's left for the Li-Ma Class is most of the words in the dictionary! This class includes nouns whose singular forms start with b, d, f, g, h, j, k, l, o, p, s, t, v, y, z! Now, not all words starting with these letters go in the Li-Ma Class, but many do.

Plural is made by adding ma- to the singular form (buku\mabuku – book).

When the ma- is added there is often a 'softening' of the first syllable. Words that begin with aspirated consonants lose the aspiration (phiri\mapiri – mountain, khutu\makutu – ear). Other 'hard' sounds are softened either by total removal of the syllable (diso\maso – eye), removal of the consonants (dziwe\maiwe – pond, bondo\maondo – knee), or by removal of the 'hard' element (dzira\mazira – egg). Sometimes no change takes place at all (dera\madera – area, bango\mabango – reed).

There are many words in this class which take only the plural form. These words are often either abstract nouns or substances rather than countable objects: mantha – fear, madzi – water, manyazi – shame, mafuta – oil.

Vocabulary:

Singular	Plural	Meaning
banja	mabanja	family
dzanja	manja	hand
dziko	maiko	country
dzina	maina	name
dzuwa	----	sun
khasu	makasu	hoe

liwu	mawu	sing. voice, vowel, pl. word, words
---	madzi	water
---	mafuta	oil
---	malo	place
---	malonda	sales, business, trade
---	mankhwala	medicine
tsamba	masamba	leaf; greens
tsiku	masiku	day

Li-Ma as subject (doer of action):

You might have wondered why this class is called the Li-Ma class. 'Sure, all the plurals begin with 'ma' but what's the 'li' part all about?' Well, here you have the answer for the 'li' part of the name:

'Li-' is the prefix to put on a verb in singular.

'A-' is the prefix to put on a verb in plural.

Tsiku likubwera. A day is coming.
Masiku akubwera. Days are coming.
Dziko lili bwino. The country is good.
Maiko ali bwino. The countries are good.

Li-Ma as objects (receivers of action)

'-lí-' for singular: Iye akulífúna banja. He wants a family.
'-ŵá-' for plural: Iye akuŵáfúna malo. He wants a place.
Ndagwira khasu. I have grabbed/am holding a hoe.
Ndaligwira. I am holding it.
Azibambo akufuna makasu. Men are looking for hoes.
Akuŵafuna. They are looking for them.

Note on 'Mfumu' (chief, king)
In singular, this word belongs in the I-Zi class, 'Mfumu ikupita.' 'The chief is going.' In plural it accords with verbs in a similar way to plurals of the Li-Ma class: 'Mafumu akupita,' etc. Respectful plural, however, adds an 'a-' prefix, 'Amfumu', 'the chief'.

6 U-Ma Class

This very small class is simple enough. It includes words beginning only with 'u-'. Plural is formed by merely adding 'ma-' to the front of the 'u-'. (uta\mauta – bow\bows)

U-Ma subjects (doers of action):
Put 'u-' on the verb for singular and 'a-' on the verb for plural:
Uta uli bwino.   The bow is good.
Mauta ali bwino.   The bows are good.

U-Ma objects (receivers of action):
Insert '-ú-' for singular and '-ŵá-' for plural:
Ndináúpeza uta.   I found the bow.
Ndináŵápeza mauta. I found the bows.

Vocabulary:

Singular	Plural	Meaning
uta	mauta	bow
ufa	---	flour
utsi	---	smoke
usiku	mausiku	night, nighttime
usana	---	daytime

(tsiku is a calendar 'day', whereas 'usana' is 'day' as

opposed to night)

Kuvuta.	To trouble, be troublesome.
Utsi unandivuta usiku.	Smoke troubled me [at] night.
Kutenga.	To take.
Ufa ndinautenga.	I took the flour.

7 Ka-Ti Class

Instead of including words that naturally begin with certain letters, this class includes all words that have had the 'diminutive prefix' 'ka-' added to them. Putting this prefix 'ka-' on the front of certain nouns makes the word mean 'a small...whatever'. Now, there is an ordinary adjective that you will learn about later that is the standard way to say something is 'small.' The prefix 'ka-' is only used on a few words. A noun with this prefix automatically goes in this Ka-Ti Class no matter what class the original word went in.
Mwana (Mu-A) – Child
Kamwana (Ka-Ti) – Small child, infant, baby

Many words that 'naturally' start with 'ka-' without a diminutive ('small') meaning will be found in the first class (Mu-A Class). (e.g. 'katundu' – stuff; 'kachewere' – white potato). Don't use every word that starts with 'ka-' as if it went in this Ka-Ti Class.

The plural for words made diminutive ('small') by adding 'ka-' is formed by:
    1. Replacing Ka- with Ti-
    2. And changing the word in its normal way to plural.

Vocabulary:

Singular	Plural	Meaning
kamwana	tiana	infant, small child
kagalu	tiagalu	puppy, small dog
kaphiri	timapiri	hill, small mountain
kamtengo	timitengo	stick, twig ('small tree')
kanthu	tinthu	something, anything

Ka-Ti subjects:

Just stick 'ka-' on the verb for singular and 'ti-' for plural:

Kamwana kakubwera. A baby is coming.

Tiana tikubwera.　　Babies are coming.

Ka-Ti objects (receivers of action):

'-ká-' for singular, '-tí-' for plural:

Ndinákáfuna kamwana.　I wanted the baby.

Ndinátífuna tiana.　　I wanted the babies.

Kuŵerenga. To read, count. Kupeza. To find.

Ife tinapeza kapepala.　We found a little piece of paper.

Tinakapeza dzulo. We found it yesterday.

Tinakaŵerenga. We read it.

Tinapeza timapepala. We found small pieces of paper.

Tinatipeza usiku. We found them [at] night.

Tinatiŵerenga. We counted them/read them.

8 Ku-

This class is made up of all verbs in their 'to' and '-ing' forms, 'to walk, walking' and 'to think, thinking'. 'Ku-' is the prefix that sits on the front of the verb stem. Of course, no plural is possible for this class. All of the verbs we have used so far could be used as examples.

kuyenda	to walk, walking
kugona	to sleep, sleeping
kufuna	to want, wanting

To use the 'ku' form of a verb as the **subject** of another verb, the doer of action, just stick an additional 'ku-' on the acting verb. To say, 'Walking will help,' we can say, 'Kuyenda kudzathandiza.'
Kufuna kuli bwino. Wanting is good.

To use a verb in its 'to' form as an **object** of a verb, use the infix '-kú-':
Kuyenda mudzákúfuna. You will want to walk.

Of course, you can always leave the particle out of the verb if you use a regular sentence order, like:
Mudzafuna kuyenda.

9 Ku-, again!

Here's another 'ku-' class, but don't be confused! The prefix 'ku-' actually has quite a lot of uses, and this is one of them. Besides meaning 'to' on a verb, it is also the preposition 'to', 'at', or 'from' on a noun. So, 'kunyumba' means 'to the house' or 'at the house.'

Kunyumba kuli bwino. At the house it's fine.

Kufika. To arrive, come.
Kunyumba kunafika anthu. To the house people came.
Virtually the same as:
Anthu anafika kunyumba. People came to the house.

Kutawuni. In town.
Kutawuni kuli nyumba. There are houses in town.
Nyumba zili kutawuni. Houses are in town.

10 Pa-

'Pa-' is a preposition meaning 'on' or 'at'. The differences between 'ku-' and 'pa-' will be discussed more later, but in short it is that 'ku-' refers to general localities, areas, directions, motion, and purpose, while 'pa-' refers to specific places, parts, and points. There's quite a lot of overlap between the two, but try to use them according to these general guidelines for now.

'Pa-' as subject:
Panyumba pali bwino.   At the house is fine.
Pampando panakhala munthu. On the chair there sat a person.
Munthu anakhala pampando. A person sat on the chair.
'Pa-' as object:
Pamalo mukupádzíŵa.   You know (on) the place.

11 Mu-

'Mu-' is the preposition 'in' and is often contracted to 'm'-' before a word.
'Mu-' as a subject:
M'nyumba muli bwino.   It's good in the house.
M'mimba muli bwino.   In the stomach is fine. (The stomach is well.) (mimba – stomach)
M'nyumba munakhala azungu. In the house there were white people/Europeans living.
'Mu-' as an object:
M'nyumba mukumúdzíŵa   You know the inside of this house.

64

Foreign Words

Words of foreign origin must be treated carefully, no matter what letter they start with. Of course, the original owners of the language didn't say things like 'kompyuta' and 'sukulu,' so when such words came in from other languages, it's understandable that they could fall kind of haphazardly into different classes. You will actually find that a lot of foreign words are used in different classes by different people!

Some foreign words are used as though they were in the 'I-Zi' Class:

sukulu	sukulu	school
galimoto	galimoto	vehicle, car
wayilesi	wayilesi	radio, radio station

Sukulu yatchipa.	School is cheap.
Sukulu zavuta.	Schools are giving trouble
Galimoto ili kugaraja.	The car is at the garage.
Galimoto zachuluka.	Cars have become too many.
(kuchuluka – to become many, too many)	

One group of foreign words could be called an 'I-Ma' Class, acting like 'I-Zi' for singular and 'Li-Ma' for plural!

kompyuta	makompyuta	computer
benki	mabenki	bank
bala	mabala	bar
gemu	magemu	game
kapu	makapu	cup
ofesi	maofesi	office
timu	matimu	team

Singular forms take i-, and plural a-:
Kompyuta ikuyaka.   The computer is running (kuyaka – to burn, be lit, run, for electrical appliances).
Makapu asoŵa.   The cups are missing.

Some foreign words go in the Li-Ma Class properly:

buku	mabuku	book
diresi	madiresi	dress
windo	mawindo	window
tchalitchi	matchalitchi	church

Diresi ndikulifuna.   I want the dress.

Some foreign words are in the Mu-A Class, singular forms only

tiyi	tea
buledi	bread
anyezi	onion
tomato	tomato
shuga	sugar
petulo	petrol
sopo	soap

Buledi ali bwino. Bread is good.
Buledi wafika. The bread has arrived.
Ndikumukonda tiyi. I love (it) tea.

Some foreign words are treated like they are in the Mu A Class in singular, but take 'ma-' for plural:

dokotala	madokotala	doctor
dalaivala	madalaivala	driver

kasitomala   makasitomala customer

Dokotala ali bwino. The doctor is fine.
Ndikumufuna dokotala. I want the doctor.
Madokotala akubwera. The doctors are coming.
but respectful, Adokotala akubwera. The doctor is coming.

Foreign words beginning with 'ch-':
cheke   macheke   check
chubu   machubu   bicycle tube
chenje   machenje   change (money)

Cheke ndikuchifuna. I want the check.
Macheke ndikuŵafuna. I want the checks.

Chapter 10: Of & Adjectives

Of

'Of' in Chicheŵa is not just a simple two-letter word like it is in English! The word 'of' shows agreement with the noun it modifies in a similar way to what we saw with verbs and nouns in the last chapter. Look at this:

Class	Chicheŵa	English
Mu A	Mwana wá John	Child of John
Mu Mi	Mutu wá mbalame	Head of a bird
Chi Zi	Chingwe chá khonje	Rope of sisal
I Zi	Nyumba yá Mada	House of Mada
Li Ma	Mafuta á ng'ombe	Fat of a cow (tallow)
U Ma	Usiku wá dzulo	Night of yesterday
Ka Ti	Kamwana ká John	Baby of John
Ku	Kuchoka kwá anthu	The leaving of the people
Ku	Kunyumba kwá Mada	At the house of Mada
Pa	Pamutu pá ine	On the head of me
Mu	M'munda mwá chimanga	In the garden of maize

Notice that the way 'of' changes with the noun classes is very similar to the way the prefix on the verb changes, except that an -a- sound is always included. In fact, the written form of 'of' is almost identical to the perfect tense prefix for the different classes, but the perfect tense prefix carries a low tone whereas this 'of' carries a high tone.

Compare: Mwana wá John. Mwana wapita.

Adjectives

Adjectives use the same particle 'of', high tone and all, to connect with nouns.

munthu wábwino – good person
anthu ábwino – good people
Tones are not normally written, but be sure to remember this
one on the adjective marker.

Vocabulary:

-bwino	good
-mbiri	many (as a noun, record, history)
-kale	before (as a noun, the past)

Mu-A Class

galu wabwino   good dog
agalu abwino   good dogs
Ndinaona munthu wamantha. I saw a fearful person.
(mantha – fear)
Anthu ambiri anali kutawuni. Many people were in town.

Mu-Mi Class

mtengo wamango   mango tree
mitengo yambiri   many trees
Dzulo ndinapita kumunda wa John. Yesterday I went to the
garden of John/John's garden.
Lero ndapita ku minda ya anthu. Today I went to people's
gardens.
Maŵa ndidzafuna mpando wa Thoko. Tomorrow I will
need/want/look for Thoko's chair.
Inu mukufuna mipeni yambiri. You (pl) want many knives.
Iwe ukufuna mpunga wambiri. You (s) want much rice.

Chi-Zi Class

chinthu chamwini   another person's thing (mwini\eni
– owner)

zinthu zakumudzi   village things ('things of at the village')

Chimanga chambiri chapita. Much maize has gone.

Kuŵerenga. To read or count.

John anaŵerenga zingwe zabwino.   John counted the good strings.

Zingwe zabwino zinali zambiri. The good strings were many.

Zingwe zabwino za John zinasoŵa.   John's good strings got lost/went missing.

Zinthu zambiri zinali mumpunga wa mayi. Many things were in mother's rice.

Akufuna chipatala chabwino. He wants (is looking for) a good hospital.

Akuchifuna chifukwa akudwala. (kudwala – to be sick.) He wants it because he is sick.

Next.../ Last...

Chaka chamaŵa	next year (literally, year of tomorrow)
Mwezi wamaŵa	next month (literally, month of tomorrow)
Chaka chatha	last year
Mwezi watha	last month

Mtengo adzaudula chaka chamaŵa. They will cut down the tree next year.

Iwo adzadula mtengo chaka chamaŵa. Same as above.

Anaudula mwezi watha.   They cut it last month.

I-Zi Class

nyumba yanjerwa	brick house (njerwa\njerwa – brick)
nyumba zamalata	houses with iron sheet roofs (lata\

70

malata – iron sheet)

Nthochi zandalama. Money bananas (grown for profit).

Ndalama zanthochi. Banana money (money from selling bananas).

Ndiwo zanyama.   Meat relish. Meat to be eaten with nsima.

Nyama zandiwo.   Animals kept for eating.

(Note: Ndiwo usually is used in the plural.)

Adzaudula mtengo nthaŵi yamvula. He will cut the tree [at] a rainy time/the rainy season.

Li-Ma Class

tsiku lakubadwa   birthday (kubadwa – to be born)

masiku akale   former days, past days

Kudziŵa. To know.   Ndikudziŵa maina a anthu. I know the names of people.

Ndikuŵadziŵa. I know them.

Ndikudziŵa dzina la munthu. I know somebody's name.

Ndikulidziŵa. I know it.

Munthu wamalonda anabwera. A seller ('person of trade') came.

Kodi malonda anali achiyani? What was he selling? Of what were the things for sale? (chiyani – what)

Anali malonda ampunga. He was selling rice. (The things for sale were of rice.)

Kodi munaugula? Did you (pl) buy it (rice)?

Ayi. No.

Chifukwa chiyani? Why?

Chifukwa wamalonda anafuna ndalama zambiri. Because the seller wanted much money. (note: 'wamalonda' is short for 'munthu wamalonda')

Kodi, iwe! Hey, you!

Unapeza masamba? Did you find greens?
Eee, ndinawapeza. Yes, I found them.
Anali a ndalama zingati? How much did they cost?
(literally: They were of money how much?) (-ngati – how much, how many)
Anali a K50. They were K50 worth ('of K50').

U-Ma Class
ufa wachimanga   maize flour
mauta akale   old bows
Usiku wabwino!   Good night!

Ka-Ti Class
kamwana kagalu   puppy, 'dog baby'
timapepala tamawu a Mulungu   gospel tracts, little
papers of the word of God

'Ku-' Class (Verbal Infinitive)
kuyenda kwamsanga   moving quickly
(msanga – fast, quick)

'Ku-' Class (To, At, From)
kunyumba kwa Phiri   at Phiri's house

'Pa-' Class
panyumba pabwino   at the good house

'Mu-' Class
m'malo mwa John   in John's place/instead of John
(malo – place)

Chapter 11: Possessive Adjectives

Possessive adjectives are words like my, your, his, their, our, etc. Although, 'mwana wa ine' (child of me), could be used to mean 'my child', there is a special form for each of the possessive adjectives in Chichewa.

-nga	my, mine
-ko	your, yours (singular)
-ke	his, hers, its
-thu	our, ours
-nu	your, yours (plural)
-wo	their, theirs

Mu-A Class

Mwana wanga.	My child.
Ana anga.	My children.
Mwamuna wako.	Your (s) husband.
Amuna ako.	Your (s) husband (respectful plural)
Mnyamata wake.	His/her boy.
Anyamata ake.	His/her boys.
Bambo wathu.	Our father.
Abambo athu.	Our fathers.
Pusi wanu.	Your (pl) monkey.
Apusi anu.	Your monkeys.
Tiyi wawo.	Their tea.

(Remember 'their' can be used for 'his/her/its' to indicate respect.)

Mu-Mi Class

Mpando wako.	Your (s) chair.
Mipeni yake.	His/her/its knives.

| Mpango wanu. | Your (pl) headscarf. |
| Miyoyo yawo. | Their lives. |

Chi-Zi Class

Zinthu zanga.	My things.
Chimfine chake.	His/her/its headcold.
Chakudya chanu.	Your (pl) food.
Zingwe zawo.	Their strings/ropes.

I-Zi Class

Nkhuku yanga.	My chicken.
Mbuzi yako.	Your (s) goat.
Ng'ombe zake.	His/her/its cows.
Nsima yanu.	Your (pl) nsima.
Nsomba zawo.	Their fish.

Li-Ma Class

Dzina langa.	My name.
Makutu ako.	Your (s) ears.
Dera lathu.	Our area. (dera\madera – area)
Mabuku anu.	Your (pl) books.
Mano awo.	Their teeth.

Ku- Verbal Class

Kuchoka kwanga.	My leaving.
Kuona kwako.	Your (s) seeing.
Kulima kwake.	His/her/its farming.
Kuzungulira kwathu.	Our going around.
Kulephera kwanu.	Your (pl) failure.
Kunyamuka kwawo.	Their leaving/starting off.

Ku- Class (To, At, From)

Kuchipinda kwanga.	To my bedroom.
(chipinda\zipinda – bedroom)	
Kumunda kwako.	At your (s) garden.
Kumalo kwake.	At His/her/its place.
Kumudzi kwathu.	At our home village.
Kumudzi kwanu.	At your (pl) home village.
Kumudzi kwawo.	At their home village.

Note: 'kumudzi' is actually a very important word meaning more or less, 'home,' indicating where one was born or where one's parents are from. Also, the singular forms ('kumudzi kwanga,' etc.) are only for the chief to say. You don't say to the average villager 'kumudzi kwako.' This is because the 'mwinimudzi' (owner of the village) is the chief. Always use the plural forms when you're referring to someone's village home. So, if you are talking about where John comes from, say, 'Kumudzi kwawo kwa John…' 'Their village of John …' (John's village). Since it is such a common idea, the word 'kumudzi' is often left off, leaving 'kwawo', their home, 'kwathu', our home, 'kwanu', your home.

Kwanu ndi kuti? Where is your home village?

Kwathu ndi ku Dedza. Our home is in Dedza.

Pa- Class

Pakhomo panga.	At my home.
Pamutu pako.	On your (s) head.
Pakhosi pake.	On his/her/its neck.
Pamudzi pathu.	At our village.
Pakhomo pawo.	At their home.

Note: 'khomo' actually means 'doorway' but finds its most important usage in the idea of 'home'. 'Pakhomo panga' differs from 'kumudzi kwathu' in that 'pakhomo panga' refers to home as the house, yard, animals and people, while 'kumudzi kwathu' refers to home as the village or district of origin. 'Kunyumba' (at the house) is almost identical in meaning to 'pakhomo'.

A common greeting is:
'Kunyumba kuli bwanji?' How's home?
'Kunyumba kuli bwino. Kaya kunyumba?' Home is fine. How is home? etc.

Mu- Class

M'sitolo mwanga.	In my store.
M'mimba mwako.	In your (s) stomach.
M'moyo mwake.	In his/her/its life.
M'nyumba mwathu.	In our house.
M'mabuku mwawo.	In their books.

Chapter 12: More Verb Tenses

We have already taken a look at the perfect tense and some forms of the past, present, and future tenses. Now I want to introduce some new forms.

-na- or -da- : Past Tense

General past action is shown by inserting the infix -ná- or -dá-, with a high tone on the same.
This is the past tense you have already learned.
Anápita ku Zomba. He went to Zomba.
Ndinámanga nyumba. I built a house.
Mulungu anátípatsa mau ake. God gave us His word.

For past actions that were interrupted or reversed by another action, the tone moves to the syllable after -na- or -da-.
Anapíta ku Zomba, koma wabwerako.
He went to Zomba, but he has come back.

Sometimes the -na- is lengthened to -naa-.
Anaamanga nyumba... He built a house...
(but then he died, or the house fell down, etc.)

-ma- or -nka- : Past Continuous Tense

Past continuous: insert infix -ma- or -nka- followed by a high tone on the very next syllable.

Next, we have past continuous or progressive action, shown by the infix '-ma-' followed by a high tone on the next syllable:

Ndimakónzekera kupíta. I was getting ready to go.
(kukonzekera – to get ready)
Amafúna kundithandiza. He wanted to help me.
Ndimachíta mantha. I was afraid.
Ndimapíta kunyumba. I was on my way home.

Sometimes the infix -nka- is used instead of -ma-.
Ndinkagwíra ntchito ku Makata. I was working at Makata.

-ma- : Habitual Tense

When the tense infix -ma- is immediately followed by a high tone, the verb is talking about continuous past action as we saw above. Change the tonal pattern on the word, and you will be describing a habitual action rather than a past progressive action.

Habitual action is shown by inserting the infix -ma- and giving the prefix before -ma- a high tone as well as a syllable or syllables near the end of the verb.

Ndímapemphéra ku Baptist. I pray at Baptist (as a habit).
(kupemphera – to pray)
Ndímadyá nsima tsiku ndi tsiku. I eat nsima daily (lit. 'day and day').
Ámathandíza kwambiri.   He helps a lot.
Ámakhála pampando waredi. He sits (usually) on a red chair.
Ndímakhála ku Bangwe.   I live in Bangwe.

78

Present Simple Tense

This tense is a bit difficult to define very precisely.

As far as form goes, it is merely indicated by the class marker directly fixed on the verb without any infix at all. The prefix takes a high tone.

Ndípita.   Chíyenda.   Madzi ábwera.   Zífika.

The verb -li is an exception as it does not take a high tone on the prefix.   Ali. He/they is/are. Chili. It is.   Ndili. I am. Zili. They are.

As far as usage or meaning goes, when it is used with most action verbs, the form holds a more or less immediate, or near, future tense.

Chípita. It will go (presently).
Chígwa. It will fall (presently, today).
Ndípita.   I will go (today, in the immediate future).
Áyenda malonda. Sales will take place (presently).
Nkhuku zífa. The chickens will die (soon).

With some verbs like -li – to be, kufuna – to want, kukonda – to love, and other similar 'abstract' verbs, this tense can be used to state a fact such as, 'I am...,' 'I want...,' 'I love...,' etc.
Ndili bwino. I am fine.
Iye áfuna madzi. He wants water.
These are basically all the same: 'I love him/her.'
Ndím'konda. Ndikumúkónda. Ndímam'kónda.

Be careful with the prefix 'a-':

Iye ápita. He will go soon.

Iwo apita. They have left. (low tone on 'a-')

The only difference is the tone which is not normally marked in writing.   If you read the word, 'Apita,' it could mean, 'They or he/she (respectful) went (lately),' or 'He/she/they will go soon.'

Future Tense

We have seen one 'future' tense already in the 'present simple' tense. But there is a proper future tense which is very straightforward. This is the future tense you learned earlier in the book. 'Adzápita', etc. When this tense is used, it indicates that the action will take place in future time, generally not immediately. It is formed by merely inserting -dzá- between the Class Marker and the stem.   'Chinthu chidzápita.' 'The thing will go.'   It corresponds in many ways to English future tense.

Nyemba zidzatha.   The beans will run out.

Bambo adzafika kunyumba. Dad will arrive at home.

Tidzadya mapeyala.   We will eat avocadoes.

Mudzaona mavuto.   You will see (experience) troubles.

Ufa udzatha maŵa. The flour will run out tomorrow.

Njala idzafika mwezi wamaŵa.   Famine will arrive next month.

Chaka chamaŵa ndidzapita kumudzi. Next year I will go to the village.

Lero ndipita kumudzi.   Today I will go to the village.

Dzulo ndinapita kumudzi. Yesterday I went to the village.

Ndafika kumudzi. I have arrived at the village.

Kale ndimakhala ku Ndirande, koma tsopano ndimakhala ku Chilomoni. Before I lived in Ndirande, but now I live in Chilomoni.

Kodi mayi, mukudya chiyani? What are you eating, ma'am?

Eee, bambo, ndikudya mbeŵa. Yes, sir, I'm eating a mouse. (mbeŵa – field mouse)

Oo? Anthu amadya mbeŵa? Oh? Do people eat mice?

Ee, anthu a ku Malaŵi amadya mbeŵa. Yes, people in Malaŵi eat mice.

Ndinamuyimbira foni dzulo. I called him on the phone yesterday. (kuyimbira foni – to call on the phone)

Kodi anayankha? Did he answer?

Ayi. Koma ndimuyimbiranso masana alero. No. But I will call him again this afternoon (the afternoon of today).

Chapter 13: Negatives

We've learned how to say something happened, is happening, or will happen. But how do we say the opposite? That something did not happen, is not happening, or will not happen? To show such an idea we can usually use the prefix 'si-' on the verb. It becomes the very first syllable on the word.

Chinthu sichikupita. The thing is not going.
Ine sindidzapita. I will not go.

Rules for negative usage:

1. If the verb prefix starts with a vowel (like 'akubwera' or 'uli bwino'), the i on si- is often dropped, letting the s- and the vowel form one syllable.
Sakubwera. He is not coming. (instead of si-akubwera)
Sali bwino. She is not fine.
Nkhuku sikubwera. The chicken is not coming. (si-i-ku-bwera = sikubwera)

2. Negative past tense changes the final '-a' of the verb to '-e'. Take special note of this.
Sindinapite. I didn't go.
Sindinafune. I didn't want.
Sanandikankhe. He didn't push me. (kukankha – to push)
Iwe sunandifune. You didn't want me.

3. The 'perfect tense' has no negative form, so just use the form of regular negative past tense:
Ndapita kutchalitchi. I have gone to church.

Sindinapite kutchalitchi. I haven't gone/didn't go to church.
Mtengo wagwa usiku. A tree has fallen in the night.
Mtengo sunagwe usiku. A tree did not fall at night.

4. The habitual tense (-ma-) often drops the -ma- when it is made negative:
Amakhala ku Lilongwe.
Sakhala ku Lilongwe.
Amamanga mbuzi ndi chingwe. She ties the goat with a rope (normally).
Samanga mbuzi ndi chingwe. She does not tie the goat with a rope.

5. The 'to' verb form uses the infix '-sa-' instead of the prefix 'si-' to show negative.
Kusadziŵa. Not to know.
Kusaona. Not to see.
Kusamva. Not to hear.
Kusapita. Not to go.
Kusathandiza. Not to help.

M'bale wake amagona m'nyumba. His relative sleeps in the house.
Sagona m'nyumba. He doesn't sleep in the house.
John akufuna njinga zambiri. John wants many bikes.
John sakufuna njinga zambiri. John doesn't want many bikes
Ndidzapita kutchalitchi maŵa. I will go to church tomorrow.
Sindidzapita kutchalitchi maŵa. I will not go to church

tomorrow.

Nkhuku zinavuta usiku.   The chickens gave trouble at night.

Nkhuku sizinavute usiku. The chickens did not give trouble at night.

Madzi avuta m'mamaŵa. The water has given trouble in the morning.

Madzi sanavute m'mamaŵa. The water didn't give trouble in the morning.

Chapter 14: Relative Tenses – After, While, Before

This section deals with the ideas expressed in such situations as:
'I went to work *while he was sleeping*.'
'I went to work *after you got back*.'
'I went to work *before he woke up*.'

While:

-KU-
The idea of 'while' is sometimes shown by the infix -ku-, like continuous present tense, but with a tonal change.
'*Ndíkúyénda*, ndinaona munthu akukwera mtengo.' 'While I was walking, I saw a person climbing a tree.'
Compare with: '*Ndikuyénda*.' 'I am walking.'
This form remains the same even when the tense of the main verb is past or future: 'Chinthu *chíkúpíta*, chinapanga ngozi.' 'While the thing was going, it had an accident.'
Note that the main verb -panga is in the past tense, therefore, we must translate '*chíkúpíta*' as 'while it *was* going,' even though its form looks like present tense.
'Adzaŵapeza *ákúpíta*.' 'He will find them while they are going.'
'Tsiku ndi tsiku ndimamudutsa iye *ákútséka* pakhomo.'
'Every day I go by while he is closing his door.'
Ndinafika *ákúpémphera* anthu. I arrived when the people were praying.

-LI

Another way 'while' is shown is by the verb -li. Look at these sentences and notice the form this basic verb takes in each case. It is always in the present tense no matter what tense verb it's referring to. The verb prefix takes a high tone.

Adzatithandiza *tíli* m'mavuto athu. He will help us while we are still in our troubles.

Amadwala kwambiri *áli* mwana. He was very sick when he was a child.

Adzapita ku Lilongwe *áli* m'mavuto. He will go to Lilongwe while he is in troubles (having trouble).

'*Áli* kulima, anaona nkhuku ikuthamanga.' 'While he was hoeing, he saw a chicken running.'

When/if:

Ngati

This word is the simplest form for expressing the idea of 'if'.

Ngati mukufuna… If you want…

Ngati iwo sapita, nanenso sindipita. If they don't go, I won't go either.

-KA-

This is used for <u>future</u> possibilities or probabilities.

Azungu akafika, ndidzakuuzani.

When/if the azungu arrive, I will tell you.

Sometimes one can use -kadza- instead of -ka-

Ndikadzabwera maŵa, ndidzakuonani.

If/when I come tomorrow, I will see you.

Zinthu zikadzakhala bwino, mudzandiona.

If things will be fine, you will see me.

Ndikachipeza ndidzakuuzani.

When I find it (chinthu) I will tell you.
Bizinesi ikadzayenda, ndidzagula galimoto chaka
chisanathe. If the business goes well, I will buy a car before
the year ends.

After:
-TA-
'After' is shown by inserting the infix '-ta-'.

Atadya nsima anaona nkhuku ikuthamanga.
After he ate nsima, he saw a chicken running.
Ndinachoka nditaona munthu akubwera.
I left after seeing someone coming.
Atadzuka, anapita kumsika.
After she woke up she went to the market.
Amapemphera atadya.
He prays after he has eaten. (his habit)
Ndipita nditapeza ndalama.
I will go after I find money.
Zinthu zidzavuta titamuona Enosi.
Things will get troublesome after we see Enos.
Zitachitika mudzamvetsa.
After they (zinthu) happen, you will understand.
Munthu amakhulupirira atamva Mau a Mulungu.
A person believes after he hears the Word of God.
Nditalemba mayeso a fomu 4, ndinapita ku Polytechnic ku
Blantyre.
After I wrote the form 4 examinations, I went to Polytechnic
in Blantyre.

-ta- can also be used like -ka- to mean 'if':
Azungu atafika, ndidzakuuzani.

If the Europeans come I will tell you.
Madzi atatha, tidzadziŵa.
If the water runs out we'll know.
Titapezeka kumeneko, zonse zikhala bwino.
If we attend there, everything will be well.

As an aside, while we are on -ta-, I should mention that -ta-
can be used to form a future perfect tense:
Maŵa tidzakhala titamaliza. Tomorrow we will have
already finished.
Mukadzafika ku Blantyre, tidzakhala titachoka. When you
do arrive in Blantyre, we will have already left.

Whenever:
-KAMA-
A combination of -ka- and -ma- habitual.
Ukamandilankhula umandisangalatsa.
Whenever you talk to me, you make me happy. (kulankhula
– to talk to; kusangalatsa – to make happy)
Zikamavuta, sindidandaula.
When things get troublesome, I don't complain.

If (past):
-KANA-
-Ka- and the past infix -na- can be joined to introduce a past
possibility. The -kana- form is found in both parts of the
sentence, the condition as well as the result.
Ndikanapita ku chipatala, ndikanachira.
If I had gone to the hospital, I would have gotten better.
Mukanandithandiza, ndikanamaliza ntchito.
If you had helped me, I would have finished the work.
(kumaliza – to finish)

88

Akanatipatsa ndalama, tikanasangalala.
If he had given us money, we would have been happy.
Ndikanakuonani, ndikanakupatsani moni.
If I had seen you, I would have greeted you.

-KADA-
An common alternate form of -kana-.
Tikadamuona, zikadakhala bwino.
If we could have seen him, things would have been good.

Before:
-SANA- -E
Insert the composite infix -sana-, and change the final -a of
the verb to -e.
Tisanafike ku Mangochi, ndinaona galimoto ya Benzi.
Before we got to Mangochi, I saw a (Mercedes) Benz car.
Bambo wanga ankagwira ntchito ku Lilongwe
ndisanabadwe ine. My father was working in Lilongwe
before I was born.
Akufuna kudzala mbeu mvula isanabwere. He wants to
plant the seed before the rain comes.

Negative When/If:
Instead of using a prefix like 'si-' on the verb, we often use
the verb 'kupanda' before the relative verb. 'Kupanda'
means 'to not' or 'to be without'.
Mukapanda kundiona mudzangopitirira.
If you don't see me, you will just keep going. (kupitirira – to
continue, go on)
Tikapanda kupeza madzi, tidzafa.
If we don't find water we will die.
Akanapanda kutiyendera, tonse tikanapita kumsika.

If he hadn't visited us, we all could have gone to the market.
Akapanda kupita ku Lilongwe, mudzandiuza.
If he doesn't go to Lilongwe, you will tell me.

Bwenzi – Then
Sometimes 'bwenzi' is used to introduce the main clause
that follows the 'if' clause.
Madzi akanapanda kupezeka kumeneko, bwenzi tonse
tikanafa.
If water had not been found there, then we all would have
died.
Tikanapitirira ulendo, bwenzi tikanakhala tafika panopa.
If we had continued the journey, we would have already
arrived by now. (ulendo\maulendo – journey)

Kupeza
The verb 'kupeza' (to find) is often found in the same
sentence with a relative tense:
Anatipeza tikudya nsima. He found us eating nsima. (He
came while we were eating.)
Anatipeza tisanadye cha madzulo. He found us before we
had eaten supper (literally, 'of evening', 'cha' is short for
'chakudya cha'). (He came before we ate supper.)
Anatipeza titachoka. He found us after we had left. (In
other words, he didn't find us at all! He came after we left.)
Anatipeza tikuchoka. He found us leaving. (He came as
we were leaving.)

Chapter 15: Verbal Adjectives

A verbal adjective is a verb used as an adjective to describe a noun. In English, if we take the verb, 'die' and put it with the noun 'man' as a verb, we get:

'The man dies.'

But as an adjective, we get:

'The dead man,' or 'The dying man.'

While it is being used as an adjective, the verb is not directly doing any action but indicating that some action was done by or happened in relation to the noun 'man'.

There are two ways to make a verb into an adjective, one way only for single syllable verbs, and another for multi-syllable verbs.

Single syllable verbs used as adjectives

The form of the verbal adjective for single syllable verbs is: *The word 'of' + the 'to' form of the verb.*

Munthu wakufa. Dead person.

Kudya. To eat. Chinthu chakudya. Thing to eat/of eating. ('Chakudya' is the most common word for 'food.')
Ndikufuna chakudya. I want food.
Kumwa. To drink.
Chinthu chakumwa. A thing to drink, or, a drink.
Munthu wakumwa madzi ali bwino. A person who drinks water is fine.
Anthu akumwa mafuta amasoẇa. People who drink oil are rare.

Multisyllable verbs used as adjectives:

Multisyllable verbs normally use a contracted prefix that turns the -aku- sound for single syllable verbs into -o-.

chaku- = cho- 'chinthu chosoŵa' – a rare thing
    (kusoŵa – to lose, not find, be missing, lost, rare)
yaku- = yo- 'njinga yokongola' – a beautiful bicycle
    (kukongola – to be beautiful)
waku- = wo- 'munthu woyendayenda' – a person who
    walks all the time, a tramp
laku- = lo- 'tsiku lobadwa' – birthday
    (kubadwa – to be born)
aku- = o- 'anthu oipa' – evil people
    (kuipa – to be bad, evil)
paku- = po- 'pakamwa potseka' – a closed mouth
    (pakamwa – mouth; kutseka – to close)
zaku- = zo- 'zingwe zoduka' – broken strings
    (kuduka – to be broken, cut)
mwaku- = mo-'m'nyengo mozizira' – in the cold season
    (nyengo – season, time period; kuzizira – to be cold)

Kusangalala. To be happy.
Munthu wosangalala. Happy person.
Anthu osangalala. Happy people.
Tsiku losangalala. Happy day (day in which to be happy).
Nthaŵi zosangalala. Happy times (times of happiness.)

Kuthamanga. To run.
Mnyamata wothamanga. A boy who runs. An athlete.
Mau othamanga. Quickly spoken words.

92

Kuvala. To wear, put on clothes.
Chovala\zovala. Clothing\clothes. (chinthu\zinthu understood)
Munthu wovala bwino. A person who dresses nicely.
Munthu wovala zovala zambiri. A person who wears lots of clothes.

Kuba. To steal. (note that this verb has a single syllable and so follows the first rule)
Wakuba \ akuba. Thief \ thieves. (standard word for 'thief')
Tinagwira akuba usiku. We caught thieves at night.
Munthu wakuba ndalama anafika kubenki.   A person who steals money came to the bank.

Kubadwa. To be born.
Mwana wa John anabadwa chaka chatha. John's child was born last year.
Ndiye mwana wobadwa chaka chatha. He is a child who was born last year (literally: 'a child of being born last year').

Note: In old books, like the *Buku Lopatulika* version of the Bible, you will find the 'waku-', 'chaku-,' 'laku-', etc. form used for all verbs, both single as well as multi-syllabic. It appears that the use of the 'o-' form (cho-, zo-, lo-, etc.) for verbal adjectives may be a rather recent development.

'Munthu' (person) and 'chinthu' (thing) are often omitted and the verbal adjective stands as a noun.

woyendetsa galimoto – driver (refers to munthu)

wophika – cook

ovuta – troublemakers (refers to anthu)

ochimwa – sinners (kuchimwa – to sin)

chovuta – problem/trouble (troubling thing, refers to the noun chinthu)

zothandiza – helpful things (refers to zinthu)

chovala\zovala – clothes

choona\zoona – truth, true

chofunika\zofunika – important thing

chakudya\zakudya – food

chakumwa\zakumwa – drink

chochita\zochita – action, something to do

      Anasoŵa chochita. He didn't know what to do.

choipa\zoipa – a bad, evil thing

cholembera\zolembera – a pen or pencil, writing instrument

chopereka\zopereka – offering (religious)

chotsala\zotsala – remain(s), leftover

chotsatira\zotsatira – result, effect

choyamba\zoyamba – first (thing in general)

'Choyamba' can be used like the English word 'first' in a speech or in writing to indicate a main point, etc.

wodwala\odwala – a sick person, patient

wogulitsa\ogulitsa – a person who sells things (this word is usually followed by what the person sells, 'wogulitsa nthochi,' etc.)

wokonza\okonza – a person who fixes things (usually followed by what he fixes, 'wokonza wayilesi', a radio repairman)

womanga\omanga – a builder

wopanda...\opanda… – a person who doesn't have or doesn't do…

wopanga…\opanga… – a person who makes…
wotsatira\otsatira – a follower, disciple
wotsogolera\otsogolera – a leader
woyimba\oyimba – a singer
woyera\oyera – a light colored person; a saint (religious)

Negative Verbal Adjectives:

The negative verbal adjective merely inserts -sa- into the
word.
Munthu wosayenda.   Someone who doesn't walk or travel
much or a lame person.
Munthu wosaona.   A blind person.
Munthu wosamva.   A deaf person.

Kufunika. To be important, helpful, necessary.
Chinthu chosafunika. An unimportant thing.
Zinthu zosafunika.   Unimportant things.
Mau osafunika.   Unimportant/inappropriate words
Dengu losafunika.   An unimportant/useless basket.

Kukoma.   To be nice, sweet, good, etc.
Nyimbo yosakoma.   A song that does not sound good.

Chapter 16: More on Ku-, Pa-, Mu-

I introduced these prepositions in the section on Noun Classes, but I left a lot to be said. These are three very important little prefixes, and they demand a more thorough look. Let's just go through pa-, ku-, and mu- again to reinforce their peculiarities.

KU-

(to)   Anapita kunyumba, kutauni, kumalo ena, etc.   He went to the house, to town, to another place, etc.

(at)   Amagwira ntchito kunyumba, kuchipatala, etc.   He works at home, at the hospital, etc.

(in)   (as used for places) in America – ku Amerika, in Europe – ku Ulaya

(from) Anachoka ku Zomba. He left (from) Zomba.
Ndimaweruka kuntchito 4 koloko. I knock off from work at 4 o'clock.   (kuweruka – to knock off)

MU- (often contracted to M'-)

(in)   Nsomba zimakhala m'madzi. Fish live in water.
       Analoŵa m'madzi. He entered the water.

(from) John anagwa m'mtengo. John fell from the tree.

PA-

(on, at) Chili pamphasa. It (chinthu) is on the mat.
Pa- might be explained as different from ku- in that it can denote a more specific point or place whereas ku- might mean a more general locality or direction, e.g. pampando (on the chair) but kunyumba (at the house) or ku Amerika.
Kumutu – toward the head (The 'head' end as opposed to

96

the 'tail' end)
Pamutu – on the head (The head itself)

Learn the differences between pa- and ku- by listening and practice. They are actually very similar and can often be used interchangeably.

Just remember this:
Pa is specific and usually has no idea of motion or direction; ku is general and sometimes has the idea of motion or direction.

'There is':

In English we like to start a lot of sentences with 'there is'. 'There is a man who…' 'There is money on the counter.' etc. This is accomplished in Chicheŵa by starting a sentence with 'kuli,' 'pali,' or 'muli', according to what fits best according to context.

Muli ndalama m'galimoto. There is money in the car.
Kuli ndalama kunyumba. There is money at the house.
Pali ndalama pathebulo. There is money on the table.

'There is not':

Instead of adding 'si-' to the front of 'pali', 'muli' and 'kuli', add '-be' to the end of the word: 'palibe,' 'kulibe' and 'mulibe'.

Mulibe ndalama m'galimoto. There is no money in the car.
Kulibe ndalama kunyumba. There is no money at home.
Palibe ndalama pathebulo. There is no money on the table.
The order of these sentences can change without

anything being affected.

M'galimoto mulibe ndalama. In the car there is no money.

etc.

Note: 'ku-' and 'pa-' are used almost interchangeably when you're making general statements in which it's not clear 'where' you're talking about. 'Pali' means literally, 'there is … on', while 'kuli' means 'there is … at', but it's appropriate to use either one when its not clear where the 'at' or 'on' is referring to. But when the context makes it clear, you should be careful to use the right one.

Parts of the Body

Some parts of the body usually come with pa-, ku-, or mu- attached to them:

pakamwa, kukamwa, m'kamwa – mouth (not just 'kamwa')

pakamwa panga – my mouth

m'kamwa mwanga – in my mouth

dzanja/manja (Li-Ma class) – hand (can be used alone, but often with m'-)

M'manja mwanga mwada. My hands are dirty. (kuda – to be black, dirty) 'Manja anga ada,' is not proper.

Kunena zakukhosi – to talk frankly, freely (literally, to say the 'from-the-neck things', i.e. words that come straight from the throat. Note: 'za' refers to 'zinthu za' 'things of'.)

Tiyeni, tikasambe m'manja! Let's go wash hands!

Tinazinyamula m'manja mwathu. We held them (zinthu) in our hands.

Ndinaima pamaso pamfumu. I stood before the chief.

(diso\maso – eye; mfumu – chief)

Pa-, Ku-, Mu- and other prepositions

Other prepositions in Chicheŵa use the prefixes pa-, ku-, and mu-.

1. -nsi – under
pansi – down, under
Pansi pathebulo… Under the table…
Pansi padziko… Under the earth…
Used as an adverb:
Kukhala pansi. To sit down.
Kuyenda pansi. To walk on foot.
Kutsika pansi. To go down. ('Kutsika' itself means 'to go down', pansi is added for emphasis.)

kunsi – down, under, at the underside
Kunsi kwa mtima… Under the heart… From the bottom of the heart…
Kunsi kwa chikwama. On the underside of the bag.

m'munsi – lower down, at the lower end
M'munsi mwa phiri – at the base of the mountain
'Munsi' can be used as a noun preceded by pa- or ku- to mean valley or lowland, i.e. not mountain e.g. kumunsiko, in the valley down there.

2. -mwamba – above, over
pamwamba – above, over
Pamwamba pamunthu… Over a person…
Pamwamba pamtengo… Over the tree…
Pamwamba pake… Above him/her/it…
Used as adverb: Kukwera pamwamba. To climb up.
Used as adjective: Chinthu chapamwamba. A better thing.

kumwamba – above, over
Kumwamba kwa dziko … Above the world…
Used to mean 'heaven': Ndidzapita kumwamba. I will go
to heaven. Kumwamba kwatsopano… A new heaven…

m'mwamba – up, above
M'mwamba mwake… Above him/her/it…
Can also mean 'sky': Mbalame zimauluka m'mwamba.
Birds fly in the sky. (kuuluka – to fly)

3. -mbuyo – behind, in the back, after
Pambuyo, Kumbuyo, M'mbuyo – behind, after
Pambuyo pagalimoto… Behind the car…
Pambuyo panga… Behind me…
Pambuyo pake, chitani ichi. After that, do this.
Kumbuyo kwathu kunali akuba sikisi. Behind us were six
thieves.
Anayang'ana kumbuyo. He looked back.
Zam'mbuyo. Things of the past.

4. -tsogolo – in front of, before
This is the opposite of -mbuyo.
Patsogolo pasukulu. In the front of the school.
Kutsogolo kwathu kunali chiphompho. In front of us was a
huge gully. (chiphompho – pit, gully, ravine)
Ndidzayamba sukulu kutsogolo. I will start (going to)
school in the future.
Akukonzekera zam'tsogolo. He's getting ready for the
future ('things of in the future').

5. -seri – behind, on the other side of objects
Paseri paphiri… On the other side of the mountain

100

Paseri pagalimoto… Behind the car
Kuseri kwa nyumba… On the other side of the house
Note: paseri and kuseri are interchangeable.
M'seri can be used to mean secretly, privately.
Anaonana m'seri.   They met/saw each other in private.
Tinachita zimenezo m'seri.   We did those things secretly.

6. -tsidya – on the other side of, on the other bank
-tsidya is different from -seri in that it is used for the other side of roads, rivers, lakes, etc., while -seri is used for buildings, mountains, and other actual physical obstructions.
Patsidya panyanja. On the other side of the river, lake.
Patsidya pamseu. Across the road.
Kutsidya kwa madzi. Over the water, on the other side.
Amakhala kutsidya.   He lives on the other side (of the local river, stream, gully, pond, lake, etc.)

7. -nja – outside of, outside
Kunja/panja are interchangeable to mean 'outside'.
Kunja kwa dziko. Outside the country.
Kunja kwa nyumba. Panja pa nyumba. Outside the house.

Kunja has some special uses:
Used as an adjective 'foreign, heathen, pagan':
      Munthu wakunja – foreigner
      Misika yakunja – foreign markets (foreign trade)
      Munthu wakunja – heathen person (religious)
      Ntchito zakunja – worldly, ungodly works (religious)

8. -kati – inside, between
-kati has no ku- form.
Pakati pa inu ndi ine. Between you and me.

Pakati pa mapiri. Between the mountains.
Pakati pa ife tonse. Among all of us.
Akukhala pakati pa ine ndi John. He is sitting in the middle between me and John.
M'kati mwanga. Inside me.
M'kati mwa nyumba. Inside the house.
Analowa m'kati. He entered inside.

Reduplications of the above used for emphasis:
m'katikati – right in the middle
Alefa anangochoka tili m'katikati mwa ntchito. Alefa just left when we were in the middle of work.
pakatikati – right in between
Nyumba yake ili pakatikati pa mapiri. His house his right between the mountains, in the very middle of the mountains.

-lipo, -liko, -limo

While we're still on pa-, ku-, mu- I should mention a very common verb. It is a combination of the being verb -li and the suffix forms -po, -ko, -mo.   It is used to mean 'is there':
-lipo, -liko, -limo

John alipo.   John is there at that place.
John aliko. John is there at that place.
John alimo. John is there in that place.

It is used in a lot of general sentences:

Bvuto lilipo/liliko. There's a problem.
Mulungu alipo/aliko.   There is a God. God exists.
Mwezi ulipo.   There is a moon.

Hale alipo? Is Harry there?

Ayi, wachoka.   No, he has gone out.

Kunyumba kunafika alendo.   Visitors came to the house.
Koma bambo kunalibe.   But father was not there.
Analiko mayi, koma sanafune kuŵaona.
Mother was there, but she didn't want to see them.
M'dengu munali tomato wambiri.   In the basket there were
many tomatoes.
Ku Ntaja kuli magetsi.   There is electricity in Ntaja.
(magetsi – electricity)
Kwathu kulibe magetsi.   At our house/place there is no
electricity.
Magetsi azima kwathu. The electricity has gone off at our
house. (kuzima – to go out of a fire, go off of electricity)
M'nyumba mwathu mulibe anthu.   There are no people in
our house.
Muli anthu ochuluka m'nyumba mwa anebala athu.
There are many people in the neighbor's house. (kuchuluka
– to be many; nebala\anebala – neighbor, from English)
Pakhosi pake sipali bwino.   His neck is not well.
Safuna kukwera galimoto, akuti ayenda pansi.   He doesn't
want to ride in a car, he says he will walk.   (kuyenda pansi
– to walk, as opposed to 'kuyenda pagalimoto')
Njoka inali pansi pankhokwe. A snake was under the
granary. (nkhokwe – granary)
Pamwamba padziko pali mlengalenga. Above the world is
the sky. (mlengalenga – sky)
Ndili pakatikati pa ulendo wanga, ndinaona mkango
pambuyo panga.   While I was in the middle of my journey,

I saw a lion behind me. (mkango\mikango – lion)
Kutsogolonso (-nso – also) kunali kambuku wamkulukulu.
In front also there was a very large leopard. (kambuku\
akambuku – leopard)
Mkati mwanga ndinachita mantha kwambiri.   Inside,
(literally: 'My inside') I was very afraid (literally: 'did
fear').
Ife timayang'ana panja pamunthu, koma Mulungu
amaonanso mkati.   We look at the outside of a person, but
God sees also the inside.

Chapter 17: To Have

In Chicheŵa we don't have a single word that means 'to have.' Instead, we use the idea of 'to be with,' just combining the verb '-li' ('to be') with the word 'ndí' ('and', 'with').

To have = to be with = -li ndi
Ali ndi ndalama. He has money.
Ndili ndi banja. I have a family.
Nyumba zathu zili ndi mavuto. Our houses have problems.

The negative is NOT made by merely adding 'si-' on the front like most verbs, rather it makes use of the '-be' suffix (similar to 'kulibe', 'palibe', and 'mulibe'):

To not have = -libe or kupanda
Alibe ndalama.   He doesn't have money.
Ndilibe banja.   I don't have a family.
Nyumba zathu zilibe mavuto. Our houses don't have problems.

Another negative for 'to have' is 'kupanda,' to not have, to be without.

This is usually used in verbal adjective forms:
Ndiwo yopanda mchere sikoma.   Relish without salt does not taste good. (kukoma – to be good, tasty)
Njinga yopanda mabuleki ikhoza kupanga ngozi. A bike without brakes can have an accident. (kukhoza – to be able, can) (ngozi – accident)

❖ ❖ ❖

Zikomo, bambo.   Excuse me, sir.
Kodi muli ndi kompyuta?   Do you have a computer?
Eee. Ndili ndi kompyuta yamphamvu. Yes, I have a
powerful computer.
Ili ndi vuto?   Does it have a problem?
Ayi, ilibe vuto.   No it does not have a problem.

Zikomo, mayi.   Excuse me, ma'am.
Muli ndi tomato?   Do you have tomatoes?
Ee, ndili ndi tomato, koma wochepa. Yes, I have tomatoes,
but few. ('Tomato' is a singular of the Mu-A class, thus the
'w' on 'wochepa.' Tomato wambiri – many tomatoes.
Tomato wabwino – could be either good tomato or good
tomatoes.)

Ine ndili ndi ndalama zambiri, koma Alefa alibe.   I have a
lot of money but Alefa does not.
Ana ali ndi vuto. The children have a problem.
Alibe madzi.   They don't have water.
Mapepala ali ndi ntchito.   These papers are useful. (literally:
'have work')
Buku langa lilibe ntchito. My book is useless.
Mau opanda ntchito. Worthless words.
Mau opanda pake. Worthless words.
Mau achabe. Worthless words. (chabe – vain, worthless,
only, just)

Chapter 18: The Being Verbs – kukhala, -li, and ndi

In Chicheŵa there are three verbs that can be translated 'to be'. Two of them are irregular verbs, very different from most other verbs in many ways. But, first, the regular one!

Kukhala

Kukhala is a general word meaning 'to be,' it can also mean 'sit,' 'stay,' or 'live.' It takes the place of the other being verbs when their irregularities keep them from being used in certain contexts or forms. Kukhala is a regular verb and can be used with all the forms, tenses and add-ons of other verbs.

But if you try to use kukhala where one of the two other being verbs (-li or ndi) would work, it will be understood under one of its OTHER meanings. For example, you've already learned 'Ndili bwino.' If you tried to say instead 'Ndikukhala bwino,' you would be understood as saying, 'I am living/staying well,' not, 'I'm fine.' In other words, kukhala takes the place of -li and ndi mostly when they can't be used due to their strange characteristics that you are just about to learn about.

-Li

-Li is used mostly for 'temporary' states or conditions such as time, health, position, and possession (remember '-li ndi', to have). It is sometimes used for permanent things as well, but, remember, its main use is for temporary states.

Ndili bwino. I'm fine.

Ndili ku Blantyre. I'm in Blantyre.

Basically, use -li only with *past tense* and the *simple present tense* form that uses the bare class marker:

Ali bwino. He's fine.

Anali bwino. She was fine.

Zili ku Zambia. They (zinthu) are in Zambia.

Unali pa windo. You (iwe) were at the window.

Negative is straightforward as in:

Sali ku Lilongwe. They are not in Lilongwe.

Sanali bwino. He wasn't fine.

Sizili kumudzi.   They (zinthu) are not in the village.

It cannot be used with:

Perfect tense, -ku- present tense form, -dza-, -ma-, ku-infinitive form, nor most other forms.   Kukhala is used where -li might need these forms.

Ndi

The verb 'ndi' is used for more **permanent** states, like names, occupation, faith, etc.

This is a very strange verb in that it takes no tense markers, and it uses no prefixes to connect to the subject. It is only used for present continuous 'being'.

John ndi munthu wabwino. John is a good person.

Madzi ndi ofunika. Water is important.

This verb can take no modifications except the the following:

When personal pronouns are the subject, the last syllable of the pronoun merges into the verb.

Ine ndine/I am, Iwe ndiwe/You are, Iye ndiye/He/she is, Ife

ndife/We are, Inu ndinu/You are, Iwo ndiwo/They are.

This can also happen with other pronouns that are discussed later:
Icho ndicho/That is, Ilo ndilo/That is, etc.

When the word that comes after the verb 'ndi' is an adjective (wabwino, zambiri, wodziŵa, lakufa), the verb 'ndi' can 'melt' into the first syllable of the adjective, but it doesn't always:

> munthu ngwabwino (ndi wabwino)
> njinga yanga njovuta (ndi yobvuta)

Notice that these are mere contractions of 'ndi' with other words and are not changes due to tense or anything of grammatical importance.

Si

The negative of 'ndi' is a lonely 'si' and it is used in basically the same way as 'ndi', except that it does not make contracted forms with the words that follow it.
Nkhuku si anthu. Chickens aren't people.
Kuyenda usiku si bwino. To walk, move at night is not good.

With the personal pronouns, 'si' does not go alone, but goes in front of the 'ndi' that sticks on the pronoun:
Ndine munthu. I am a person.
Sindine munthu. I am not a person. (Then how are you so good at Chicheŵa?)
Ndiwe mnyamata. You (s) are a boy.
Sindiwe mnyamata. You (s) are not a boy.

To summarize:

'-Li' can use these forms:
Simple present: as in, ali, zili, chili, lili, ili, ali, uli, pali, kuli, muli, etc.

Simple past: as in, anali, zinali, chinali, linali, panali, kunali, munali, etc.

Negative simple present: as in sali, sizili, sichili, sili, sali, palibe, kulibe, mulibe, etc.

Negative simple past: as in sanali, sizinali, sichinali, panalibe, kunalibe, munalibe.

For health, condition, position and other temporary states:
Ndili bwino. I'm fine.
Muli wosangalala. You are happy.
Zili kunyumba. They (zinthu) are at the house.

'Ndi' uses:
Only present: ndi, ndine, ndiwe, *ndicho, ndizo, ndilo,* ngwabwino, nchovuta, etc. (note: italicized forms refer to pronouns that haven't been introduced yet.)

Negative present: si, sindine, sindiwe, si wabwino, si lovuta, si chosôwa.

For permanent states:
Ndine John. I am John.
Ndine munthu. I am a human.
Ndi nkhuku. It is a chicken.
Ndi chovuta. It is troublesome.
Ndi chabwino. It is good.

'Kukhala' takes up the slack where needed:
Command: Khalani omvera! Be obedient! (kumvera – to obey)

Verbal adjectve: Wokhala mphunzitsi.   One who is a teacher.

And any other use of 'is/be':

Asanakhale bambo… (Before he was a father…)

Zitadzandikhalira choncho! If things would only be like that for me! (And you were starting to think Chicheŵa was easy!)

'Still,' 'When still' -kali, -kadali, -dakali

The being verb -li has some interesting ways of showing the idea of 'is still' or 'when … was still'.

-kali (still)

Ndikali wamng'ono. I am still young.

-dakali or -kadali (still)

Sindiseŵera ndi John; akadali mwana. I don't play with John, he's still a child.

Adakali ku Mangochi. He's still in Mangochi.

-be (still, yet) can be added for more emphasis.

Ameneyo akadali moyobe. That guy is still alive.

Sara akadali mwanabe. Sarah is still a child.

-dakali or -kadali (when … still)

Ankagwira ntchito adakali bwino. She used to work when she was well.

Anali munthu wamkulu adakali moyo. He was a big man while he was alive.

Amayi anamwalira ndikadali mwana. Mom died when I was young. (kumwalira – to die)

❖ ❖ ❖

John ali ku Dedza.   John is in Dedza.
John ndi wakuba.   John is a thief.
John adzakhala pamavuto.   John will be in trouble.
(literally, 'on troubles')

Maria ali pamavuto.   Mary is in trouble.
Maria ndi mwana wamfumu.   Mary is the chief's daughter.
Maria adzakhala bwino.   Mary will be all right.

Dzina lanu ndani?   What is your name?   (Note: 'ndani' is
actually a contraction of 'ndi yani', even though it is often
considered a single word meaning 'who')
Dzina langa ndi Yonasi.   My name is Yonasi.
Dzina lake la mwana wanu ndani?   What is the name of
your child?   (Literally: 'His name of your child is who?')
Dzina lake ndi Tomasi.   His name is Thomas.

Aphunzitsi ali bwino.   The teachers are fine (not sick).
Aphunzitsi ndi abwino.   The teachers are good teachers.
Aphunzitsi anali abwino.   The teachers were good teachers.
Aphunzitsi okhala abwino adzabwera.   The teachers who
are good will come.   (Note: 'kukhala' is used because 'ndi'
and '-li' cannot be used with the verbal adjective (-o-) form.)

Chapter 19: Double-Prefix Adjectives

chinthu chaching'ono	(small thing)
chinthu chachikulu	(large thing)
chinthu chachitali	(long thing)
chinthu chachifupi	(short thing)
chinthu chachikazi	(female thing)
chinthu chachimuna	(male thing)
chinthu chachiŵisi	(fresh thing)

The members of this very small but important group of adjectives connect with nouns using a double prefix. In order to use one of these adjectives, we use two prefixes, the form of the first is like the regular adjective prefix and the second like the regular verb prefix.

-kulu (big) Chinthu cha-chi-kulu. Big thing.

'Cha-' as in 'chabwino,' '-chi-' as in 'chikupita.'

-ng'ono (small) Chinthu chaching'ono. Small thing.

Mpando waung'ono. Small chair.

Mipando yaing'ono. Small chairs.

Zinthu zazing'ono. Small things.

Unfortunately enough, the Mu-A class has a slight quirk when being used with these words. It puts an -m- for the second prefix in singular.

Munthu wamng'ono. Mwana wamkulu. etc.

The double-prefix adjectives are not really very numerous, but, as you can see, some of them are very important.

-ng'ono (small) Mwana wamng'ono. (Small child.) Vuto laling'ono. (Small problem.)

-kulu   (large) Chala chachikulu. (Big finger.) Mapiri aakulu. (Big mountains.)

-tali   (long) Munthu wamtali. (Tall person.) Nsomba zazitali. (Long fish.)

-fupi   (short) Kamtengo kakafupi. (Short stick/tree.) Chingwe chachifupi. (Short string.)

-kazi   (female) Mwana wamkazi. (Daughter.) Agalu aakazi. (Female dogs.)

-muna (male)   Mbuzi zazimuna. (Male goats.) Mwana wamwamuna. (Son.)

Note: The word '-muna' is an exception to the rule in that when it is used with singular Mu-A class, it takes this form: 'wamwamuna.' The word is regular for all other forms.

-ŵisi   (fresh, green, not cooked, or not ripe.)   Papaya laliŵisi. (unripe papaya.) Nyemba zaziŵisi.   (Undried beans.)

Mwana wamng'ono anapeza kagalu kakang'ono panjira. A little child found a little puppy on the path.

Munthu wamkulu amakwera galimoto yaikulu. A big person rides (literally: climbs in) a big vehicle.

Mayi anabereka mwana wamkazi wamkulu. Mother gave birth to a big female child (girl).

Mayi anabereka kamtsikana kakakulu. Mother gave birth to a big baby girl (little girl).

Anthu ambiri ndi aafupi kwambiri. Many people are very short.

Zomba ndi phiri lalitali komanso lalikulu.   Zomba is a tall and large mountain. (komanso – but also, and)

Chapter 20: -Ka- and -Dza-

These are two unique infixes that are often used to modify verbs. They go right after the tense marker in the verb. Akukafuna, anadzadya, etc. -Ka- often means to 'go and do' and -dza- means to 'come and do.' So, if -ka- is used in a past tense verb with 'John' for the subject, it would be translated as 'John went and did ...'

John anakadya kunyumba kwa aPhiri.
John went and ate at the house of the Phiris.

Ka

Carries the idea of 'go and do...' or 'go to do...'
Anakagona ku Lilongwe. He went and slept in Lilongwe.
Tidzakapemphera ku tchalitchi. We will go and pray at church.
Anapita kukadya.   He went to eat.
Anakadya.   He went and ate.
Munakachita chiyani? What did you go do?
Ku Malonje ndidzakapeza chakudya. I will go find food at Malonje.
Ndidzakagula zovala kumsika. I will go buy clothes at the market.

Dza

The infix -dza- can mean 'come and do' or 'come to do'.
Ndabwera kudzathandiza. I have come to help.
Ndinadzam'peza kuno. I came and found him here.

Kutani? To do what?

115

Mukutani? What are you doing?

Ku Mangochi munakatani? What did you go and do in Mangochi?

Tinakagula nsomba zaziŵisi. We went and bought fresh fish.

Munabwerera kuno ku Zomba chifukwa chiyani? Why did you come back here to Zomba? (kubwerera – to return, come back)

Tikudzafunafuna ntchito. We are coming to look for work. (kufunafuna – look for)

Chalo anadzandithandiza. Chalo came and helped me.

Kodi munakaphunzira kusukulu dzulo? Did you go learn at school yesterday?

Ayi, tinakaseŵera mpira. No, we went and played football. (kuseŵera – to play) (mpira – football, soccer)

More on -ka-

The infix -ka- is sometimes used as a tense marker to form what might be called 'near future tense'. The sense sometimes seems to be that the action will take place in relation to or dependent on something else. It might presuppose an unspoken conditional -ka- (if) clause.

Mukandipeza kuntchito. You will find me at work (when you come).

Zikavuta kumsonkhano. Things will get bad at the meeting (if such and such happens).

About, 'za'

This small but important word usually takes the place of the English 'about.' It is really the 'of' form that follows the word 'zinthu' (zinthu za munthu, etc.)

116

'Za' follows words like kunena (to say), kulankhula (to speak), kuuza (to tell), kufunsa (to ask), kumva (to hear), kumvetsa (to understand), kuzindikira (to know, realize), and kudziŵa (to know).

Ndinamva za Yohane. I heard about John.

Amakonda kudandaula za mavuto ake.   He likes to complain about his problems. (kudandaula – to complain)

Chapter 21: -Mene and -Mwe

These two very important words are basically identical in meaning and usage. They can be used to express the English relative pronouns: *which, who, where,* and *when.* Note that these are not used as question words but only as relative pronouns. 'The man *who* was here...' 'I went *where* no one else was.'

-Mene is always used with a prefix, the same as the verb prefix.
chinthu chimene..., the thing which...
munthu amene..., the person who...
zinthu zimene..., the things that...
nyumba imene..., the house which...
pakhomo pamene..., on the porch where...

-Mwe uses the prefixes that work with the verbal adjectives (cho-, zo-, o-, lo-, etc.).
madzi omwe..., the water that...
phiri lomwe..., the mountain which...
njinga zomwe..., the bicycles that...

As far as form, -mwe has one exception, for the Mu-A class (words like munthu) don't use 'womwe' but use 'yemwe'!
munthu yemwe..., bambo yemwe..., etc.
For plural, it is 'anthu omwe' as expected.

-Mene and -mwe are interchangeable:
'Chinthu chimene' = 'Chinthu chomwe'.

Who, which, that

When used after a noun, these words are like 'which,' 'that' or 'who'.

Chinthu chimene chili pathebulo… Chinthu chomwe chili pathebulo… The thing that is on the table…

Anthu amene amagula ufa… Anthu omwe amagula ufa… The people who buy flour …

Munthu amene ndikumufuna wachokapo. The person whom I want has left.

Where, when

'Where' and 'when' are merely the forms of -mene and -mwe that have 'pa-,' 'ku-' or 'mu-' on front of them.

pamene	kumene	m'mene
pomwe	komwe	momwe

Kumudzi kumene anthu achita bwino kwambiri ndi ku Sondo. The village where people did very well is Sondo village.

Tinayenda m'njira m'mene munali mavuto ambiri. We traveled in a path in which there were many troubles.

Note: any of these sentences could have the -mwe form instead of the -mene form, and the converse is true for the sentences below:

Pakhomo pathu ndi pomwe anthu ambiri amafikafika. Our home is the one many people come repeatedly to (kufikafika – come repeatedly).

Komwe kuli nsomba kuli madzi. Where there are fish there is water.

These forms (pamene, pomwe, kumene, komwe, m'mene, and momwe) can be used alone as 'where' and 'when':

Tidzasangalala pamene tidzaona John. We will be happy when we see John. ('pamene' might refer to an unspoken 'panthaŵi')

Kumene mukupita kuli mavuto. Where you are going there are troubles.

M'mene timachoka ku Blantyre, sitimakudziŵani. When we were leaving Blantyre, we didn't know you (yet).

As a general rule:

Pamene and m'mene used alone can mean 'when'.

Pamene, Kumene, and M'mene can all be used to mean 'where', depending on the context.

How – m'mene, momwe

The mu- forms of -mene and -mwe can also be used where the English 'how' would be used.

When used in this way, the verb takes a -ra ending.

Ndimafuna kuona m'mene amachitira. I wanted to see how he does (it).

Ndinam'funsa za m'mene amagŵirira ntchito. I asked him about how he works.

With -li, instead of adding a -ra ending, merely reduplicate the -li:

Zinthu sizili bwino m'mene zilili. Things aren't fine how they are.

Relative clauses without -mene or -mwe

Using -mene or -mwe is not the only way to use relative clauses (clauses involving *who, which, that, where,* etc.).

Sometimes the word 'who' or 'which' is completely left out

120

but the verb still takes the intonation of a relative clause. This is very common in sentences involving the being verb 'ndi'.

John ndiye amapita. John is the one who goes.

Ali bwino ndiye.   The one who is well is he.

Ndikufuna kupita ndine. I am the one who wants to go.

Another Use of -Mene and -Mwe

These two words are not only used as relative pronouns (who, where, when, how) but also to mean 'even' or 'as well' or 'also,' as in the following sentences:

He looked everywhere, in the kitchen, in the granary, and *even* in the [animal] pen.

Anayang'ana monsemonse, mukitcheni, munkhokwe ndi mukhola momwe. (monsemonse – in every place; nkhokwe\ nkhokwe – granary; khola\makola – animal pen, kraal)

He came with his wife *as well.*

Anabwera pamodzi ndi mkazi wake yemwe. (pamodzi – together)

Everything burned up—his bike, his bed, his books, and his toothbrush *also!*

Zonse zinapsya—njinga yake, bedi yake, mabuku ake, ndi mswachi wake womwe! (zonse – all things; mswachi\ miswachi – toothbrush)

Kuthaŵa. To run away.   Nyama zapakhomo zinathaŵa. The animals at home ran away.

Ndi nkhuku zomwe zinathaŵa.   Even the chickens ran away.

Nkhuku zambiri zinapita kuthengo, ndi kulôwa m'phiri
momwe.
Most of the chickens went to the bush, and even 'entered
into (went up) the mountain'. (thengo – bush, wild area)

Ndalama zimene ndinakupatsani ndi zambiri.
The money that I gave you is a lot.

Kiri ndi mwana amene sasôwa chochita.
Kiri is a child who doesn't lack something to do.

Amene amafuna kuphunzira anabwera.
Those who wanted to learn came.

Phiri lalikulu limene lili ku Malaŵi ndi Mulanje.
The large (largest) mountain which is in Malaŵi is Mulanje.

Tinadzafunsa za makasu omwe akupezeka kuno.
We came and asked about the hoes that are available here.
(khasu\makasu – hoe; kupezeka – to be found, available;
kuno – here)

Akuba anabwera usiku ndipo anatenga katundu wa pano,
ndi makasu omwe.
Thieves came at night and they took the stuff from here,
including even the hoes. (wakuba\akuba – thief)

Anabwera kunyumba kudzafunsa za m'mene mulili inu.
He came to the house to ask about how you are.

Anadabwa ataona m'mene zimayendera.
He was amazed after he saw how things go/work.

Chapter 22: This and That, Here and There

'This, that, these, those, here, there.' That was only six words, but in Chicheŵa, there are several *hundred* word forms that take the place of this small list of English demonstratives!

This

There are basically two words for 'this'.
1. Chinthu ichi. This thing, the one near me, or the one I just mentioned. I might even be pointing at it.
2. Chaka chino. This year, the one we are in, the stem '-no' indicates that you are engulfed by the thing you are referring to.

Of course, in the examples here I just gave the forms as they appear for the Chi Zi class singular. Below is a list of both 'this' words for all the classes, singular and plural. The singular form indicates, 'this', while the plural, of course, means, 'these.'

'This' Demonstratives

Class Name	This 1 (pointing)	This 2 (engulfing speaker)
Mu-A	munthu uyu azungu aŵa	-----
Mu-Mi	mtedza uwu mitengo iyi	mwezi uno/miyezi ino [mwezi – month]
Chi-Zi	chinthu ichi zinthu izi	chaka chino zaka zino

I-Zi	nyumba iyi ng'ombe (cattle) izi	nyengo ino (this season) nthaŵi zino
Li-Ma	diso ili (this eye) madzi aŵa	dziko lino (this country) masiku ano (these days)
U-Ma	ufa uwu (this flour) mausiku aŵa	usiku uno mausiku ano
Ka-Ti	kabuku aka timabuku iti	kanyumba kano tinyumba tino
Ku	kufika uku (this coming, arrival)	-------
Pa	pakhomo apa	pakhomo pano
Ku	kuphiri uku (here at the mountain)	ku Zomba kuno
Mu	m'thumba umu (in this pocket, bag)	m'madzi muno

Most of the time, the first 'this' demonstrative (the 'pointing' form) likes to merge itself onto the end of the noun it modifies.

munthu uyu ---> munthuyu
anthu aŵa ---> anthuŵa
mtengo uwu ---> mtengowu
mitengo iyi ---> mitengoyi
chinthu ichi ---> chinthuchi
nyumba izi ---> nyumbazi
dziko ili ---> dzikoli
kuphiri uku ---> kuphiriku

Both of these 'this' words love to get stuck on the end of -mene and -mwe.

'Chinthu chimenechi' is basically the same as 'chinthuchi'. It's just a little more emphatic or 'colorful.'

munthu ameneyu
anthu omwewâ
zinthu zomwezi
nyumba zimenezi
lero lomweli
nyumba yomweyino
lero lomwelino
chaka chimenechino
pakhomo pomwepano

Here

Uku, apa, umu, kuno, pano, and muno all mean 'here' (ie. this place) depending on their exact form.

Uku means 'here' (in this direction)
Tinapita uku. We went this direction.

Kuno means 'here' (in this area, speaker is included in the area described by 'kuno')
Ndinabwera kuno. I came here.

Apa means 'on here' (on this spot, at this place, the spot the speaker is talking about, but not where the speaker is)
John amakhala apa. John stays here, where I'm pointing.

Pano means 'on here' (on this spot, at this place, where I am)
John amakhala pano. John stays right here, where we are.

There is actually some overlap between the various forms so don't get the impression that you have to be scientifically accurate.

Of course, the following forms are very common and the principles of usage I just mentioned apply to these forms as well. All of the following mean 'here.'
Pamenepa, Pomwepa, Pamenepano, Pomwepano
Kumeneku, Komweku, Kumenekuno, Komwekuno
M'menemu, Momwemu, M'menemuno, Momwemuno

Some common colloquial contractions of the above are:
Pompa (from pomwepa) – on this place
Pompano (pomwepano) – on this place where I am
Konkuno (komwekuno) – at this place where I am
Mommu (momwemu) – in here
Mommuno (momwemuno) – in here where I am

Padakali pano/Pakadali pano/Pakali pano
A common phrase is 'padakali pano' or 'pakadali pano', meaning 'at this time,' or 'at this point.' It usually follows a story or comes as the conclusion of a point.
Padakali pano, anthu akumamuseka mwanayo. Now, people are laughing at that child.
(The mixing of -ku- and -ma-, 'Akumamuseka', indicates merely that the response of the people to the child is always that of laughing, not that they are laughing at this exact moment.)
Pakali pano, mwanayu ali kuchipatala. Now, this child is at the hospital.

That

The two basic words for 'that' in the Chi-Zi class (just to demonstrate) are:

1. Chinthu icho. That thing, that I'm pointing at or referring to. Zinthu izo. Those things. Contrast *ichi – this* and *icho – that*.

2. Chinthu chija. That thing, one referred to previously in speaking, or, that thing known to all parties. Zinthu zija. Those things (you know, previously mentioned).

'That' Demonstratives

Class Name	That (ordinary, pointing)	That ('the one you know')
Mu-A	mphunzitsi uyo (that teacher) ana awo (those children)	mtsikana uja (that girl) anyamata aja (those boys)
Mu-Mi	mpando uwo miyendo iyo (those legs)	moyo uja (that life) mitengo ija
Chi-Zi	chingwe icho zovala izo (those clothes)	chaka chija zaka zija
I-Zi	ndege iyo (that plane) njira izo (those ways)	mvula ija (that rain) mbewu zija (those seeds)
Li-Ma	bodza ilo (that lie) magulu awo (those groups)	dera lija (that area) masiku aja

U-Ma	usiku uwo (that night) mausiku awo	ufa uja mauta aja (those bows)
Ka-Ti	kamwana ako (that small child) timabuku ito (those small books)	kanyumba kaja tinyumba tija
Ku	kubwera uko	kubwera kuja
Pa	pakhomo apo	pakhomo paja
Ku	ku Zomba uko	ku phiri kuja
Mu	m'nyumba umo	m'madzi muja

Just like with the 'this' demonstratives, the ordinary, or 'pointing', 'that' likes to hitch a ride on the end of the word it refers to.
munthuyo
pakhomopo
chinthucho
zinthuzo
nyumbayo
kamwanako

Also, just like with the 'this' demonstrative, -mene and -mwe love to be used with both of the 'that' demonstratives, without adding much to the meaning:
munthu ameneuja (that man, the one you know)
munthu ameneyo (that man)
chingwe chimenecho (that string, rope) etc.
chingwe chomwechija
nkhuku zomwezo
malo omweaja

128

There

Of course, 'there' is just the pa-, ku-, mu- forms of 'that':

apo, uko, umo – on there, to there, in there

paja, kuja, muja – on there, to there, in there ('you know the place')

pamenepo, kumeneko, m'menemo

pamenepaja, kumenekuja, m'menemuja

pomwepo, komweko, momwemo

pomwepaja, komwekuja, momwemuja

All of the above mean 'there', with possible slight variations in meaning according to their precise form.

Below are some very common contracted forms for the word 'there'.

pompo (pomwepo) – there, on that spot, that I'm pointing/ referring to

pompaja (pomwepaja) – there, on that spot, that you know where it is

konko (komweko) – there, at that place, that I am pointing/ referring to

konkuja (komwekuja) – there, at that place, that you already know about

mommo (momwemo) – in there, into which I'm pointing/ referring to

mommuja (momwemuja) – in there, you know where (didn't I tell you before?)

Demonstratives and the word 'ndi'

When the short forms (uyu, aŵa, ili, iyi, ichi, etc.) are used after the word 'ndi', a combination can take place. If 'ndi' is being used as the verb 'to be', the combination takes one form, but if the word is being used as 'with' or 'and' then the form will be still another.

'Ndi' as a verb:
Ndi iwo. It is them. > Ndiwo. It is them.
Ndi icho. It is that. > Ndicho. It is that.
Ndi izo. It is those. > Ndizo. It is those.

'Ndí' as 'with' or 'and':
Kuyenda ndi iwo. To travel with them. Kuyenda nawo.
Ali ndi izo. He has them. Ali nazo.
Ndikufuna ndikhale ndi icho. I want to have that.
Ndikufuna ndikhale nacho.
Ndikhale nawo anthuŵa. Let me live with these people.
Ayende nazo ndalama. He should travel with money.
Kompyuta ndi yofunika kukhala nayo. A computer is important to have.

This, that as who, which
The demonstrative pronouns (this, that) can be used in place of who, which:
Akuyenda apoyo ndi mbale wanga. He is going over there (that one) is my relative. In other words: The one who is going over there is my relative.
Anapita ku Blantyre uja ndi mbale wanga. The one who went to Blantyre is my relative.
Kodi zinathandiza zija zilipobe? Are the things that helped (back then) still around?
Nkhumba ija imabereka ana ambiri ndi iyi. This is the pig that has a lot of babies (the one you heard about already).
Ndikumufuna uja ali apo, koma ndaona kuti athanganidwa kwambiri. The person that I want is over there, but I've

130

seen that he's very busy. (kuti – that)

Buku ili ndi lofunika kwa anthu ophunziraŵa.   This book
is important for these educated people. (kufunika – to be
wanted, important)

Anthu ameneŵa anaona nyumba zoonongeka zija.   These
people saw those ruined houses (the ones formerly
mentioned).

Nyama zinazo sindimazikonda.   Those other meats I don't
like.

Nyama yabwino ndiyo.   That's the good meat.

Nayo nyama ya nkhuku ndi yabwino.   Even ('also it')
chicken meat is good.

Akufuna madziwo; ali nawo cholinga.   He wants that water;
he has a purpose for it.

Mkaka wokomawu tikuugulitsa pamtengo womweuja wa
K50.   This good tasting milk we are selling it at that same
price (the one you heard before) of K50. (kukoma – to be
nice, tasty, pleasant; kugulitsa – to sell; mtengo – price)

Chapter 23: Commands, Wishes, and Possibilities

You probably needed this section a long time ago. One can't go very long without asking or telling someone else to do something.

Imperative:

The basic way to make a command to 'you' is to just say the verb with no prefixes or suffixes:

Bwera! Come!
Choka! Go away!

This is very similar to English. ('Come!' 'Go!') But **this form is actually singular (iwe – you, singular) and is considered disrespectful**.

Adding -ni to the verb makes the **plural and respectful command form, which is the form for general use in most situations**.

Bwerani. Come.
Siyani. Leave (it).
Chokani! Go away!
Ŵerengani. Read.

Ŵerengani Baibulo tsiku ndi tsiku. Read the Bible every day. (tsiku ndi tsiku – every day; literally, day and day).
Yendani bwino. Travel well.
Pitani bwino. Go well.
Gonani bwino. Sleep well.
Dziŵani chimenechi. Know this.
Samalirani moyo wanu. Take care of your life.

Ta-...!

A common, but less formal command form adds 'ta-' to the front of the previous form.

Tabwerani. Come.

Tapita! Go! (iwe)

Iwe, tapita! You, go! (Get out of here!)

Tabwera kuno! Come here!

Tachokani pano! Get out of here!

Taŵerengani nyuzi iyi. Read this newspaper. (nyuzi – newspaper)

Wish:

To make more of an indirect command or a request, change the last vowel '-a' to '-e', still making use of the proper prefixes, but no tense markers.

Mupite. You should go. Please go.

Ubwere maŵa. You should come tomorrow.

To tell someone that someone else must do something, this is the form to use.

'Let him come,' is 'Iye abwere.'

This form can be used for any class of noun or any personal pronoun: Chipite. Zione. Iwe uyende. Etc.

It can also be used in a question like, 'Ndibwere?' 'Should I come?'

The negative form is shown by inserting the infix -sa- following the class marker:

Asabwere maŵa. He shouldn't come tomorrow.

Ndisam'patse ndalama. I shouldn't give him money.

Nkhuku zisagone muno. The chickens shouldn't sleep in here.

This form, or forms derived from it, will often be used when the command includes an infix such as an object personal pronuoun or -ka-, -dza-,etc.
Mundipatse. Give (it) to me.
Mukapezeke kumeneko. You should go attend there.
(kupezeka – to be found, present, attend)

This form can also be used in a word that follows 'kufuna' instead of the 'to' form of the verb:
Ndikufuna ndipite. I want to go. Same as, 'Ndikufuna kupita.'
Amafuna apeze nyumba. He wanted to find a house. Same as, 'Amafuna kupeza nyumba.'

Andipatse ndalama. Let him/may he/he should give me money.
Ndikaone zimene zikuchitika. Let me go/I should go see what is happening.
Musanene mau aŵa. You shouldn't say these words.
Tisamenyane. Let us not/we should not fight. (kumenyana – to fight)
Nsomba zisathawe. The fish shouldn't escape. (kuthaŵa – to run away, escape)
Agalu athamangitse akuba. Let the dogs/The dogs should chase the thieves. (kuthamangitsa – to chase)

Must (habit or general requirement): -zi-
A form that can be used in a similar way to the -e ending above is the insertion of the -zi- infix.

134

Muzipita. You should go. You must go.

Ana aziŵerenga kaŵirikaŵiri. Children should read often.

Should: -yenera

Muyenera kupita. You should go.

Muyenera mupite. You should go.

Tiyenera kupemphera kwa Mulungu. We should pray to God.

The verb -yenera is followed by the infinitive ('to' form) or subjunctive ('-e' form) of the action verb. 'Kuyenera' is treated like a regular verb and must have appropriate prefixes and infixes connected to it.

Ayenera kupita. He should go.

Anayenera kupita. He should have gone.

Adzayenera kupita. He will have to go.

This verb is actually also a stand-alone verb with the meaning 'be worthy of'.

'Yesu ayenera ulemu.' 'Jesus is worthy of honor.'

Simuyenera kubwera kunyumba kwathu. Can be taken as, 'You don't have to come to our house,' or, 'You shouldn't come to our house.'

Commands in mixed form:

Many mixed or altered forms will be encountered. The colloquial expressions of command are almost endless, it seems. On some of them, certain parts are dropped off while others are mixtures of different command forms. Common examples are given below, most are in the second person plural unless otherwise noted.   This is not for you to try to memorize at first, but just to get you started on your own exploration of colloquial forms.

Kaoneni!   Go see! (Note that the -ka- infix makes the verb carry the -e on the end and yet there is also the -ni of the imperative!)
Muzimapita!   You should (always) go! (habit)
M'patseni!   Give it to him! (Again the '-mu-' infix for 'iye' makes the verb carry the -e of the subjunctive and yet the first prefix that we would expect (Mu- for 'inu') is dropped and instead there is the -ni of the imperative.)
Kam'patseni! Go give it to him!
Muzikam'patsa!   You should go give it to him!
Patseni ndalama. Give me money.
M'patseni mzimbe. Give him sugar cane.
Tipatseni zomwezo. Give us the same stuff.

Negative:
The negative for commands is the infix '-sa-' with the '-e' ending.
Musapite.   Don't go.
Asaone zimenezi.   They shouldn't see these things.

With '-ma-' the final '-e' changes back to its ordinary '-a'.
Musamayenda kutali. Don't go far (regularly).

Another very common negative form is 'osa-' with the regular '-a' ending.
Iwe, osapita kumeneko! You, don't go there!
Inu, osabwera pano!   You, don't come here!
Osaganiza kuti tikupatsani ndalama. Don't think we'll give

you money.

Tapitani kuphiri, mukatenge nkhuni.   Go to the mountain and get firewood. (nkhuni – firewood)
Muyenera kulapa machimo anu.   You should repent of your sins. (kulapa – to repent)
Lapa machimo ako!   Repent of your sins!
Talapani! Repent!
Musakwere mtengo, mungagwe. You shuoldn't climb the tree, you could fall.
Musamakwera mitengo. You shouldn't climb trees. (note the final -a due to the inclusion of -ma-)
Kamuitaneni!   Go call him!
Dzaŵaone!   Come see them! (Shortened from 'Iwe udzaŵaone iwo!')
Azidzationa ife.   He should come see us.
Patseni madzi akumwa. Give me drinking water.
Ndipatseniko madzi akumwa.   Give me some water to drink. (-ko on the verb makes the command more polite)

Chapter 24: Please

'Chonde' is often considered the direct translation of 'please'. Indeed, 'chonde' replaces 'please' in a lot of situations. 'Chonde, ndithandizeni!' 'Please help me!'

However it is a word that does not so much have polite connotations but forceful pleading connotations.

Politeness is indicated by indirectness. For an example of the indirectness principle, we learned earlier that when talking to someone, we should always address them with a plural 'you', or even call them 'they' to their face for extra politeness. Make it a habit to use a more or less indirect way of making requests.

Requesting for permission:

Nawo – 'with them'
Ndimwe nawo madzi.   May I drink water with them?
Nditsike nawo pa siteji.   May I get off (the minibus) with them at the stage? (Even though you are the only one getting off.)
Ndingamenye nawo mpira?   Can I play ball with you?
Mayi, ndingadutse nawo?   Ma'am, can I pass?   (i.e. 'Excuse me.')
A good introductory word for some situations like the above is either 'Pepani' or 'Zikomo.'
'Zikomo, ndingadutse nawo?' 'Excuse me, can I pass?'
'Pepani, ndadutsa.'   'Sorry, I am passing.' ('I have passed.')

-ko, -po

Besides their ordinary prepositional meaning of 'there', these particles on the end of a verb can soften the verbs force (Aliko bwino. He's a little better.), thus, when the verb is being used as a command, it softens the command, making it more polite.

Ndipatseniko madzi.   Give me a little water.

Sometimes the -ni follows the -ko.

Thandizekoni!   Please help me!

Other 'indirect' words, like 'pang'ono', work in the same way:

Kodi ndingacheze nanu pang'ono?   May I chat with you a little?

More polite requests:

Kodi mungasangalatsidwe kubwera nafe?   Would you be pleased to come with us? (kusangalatsidwa – to be pleased)

Kodi mungandithandizeko pang'ono?   Could you help me a little bit?

Kodi mungandithandizeko ndi ndalama? Can you help me with money?

For even more respect use the forms 'iwo' and 'a-':

Zikomo, amfumu! Kodi angatiperekeze kutawuni?   Excuse me, chief! Can you (lit. they) accompany us to town?

Pepani, agogo! Tingagawe nawo pang'ono Mau a Mulungu? Sorry, grandfather! Can we share with you (lit. them) a little the Word of God?

Chapter 25: Questions

Sentence Order

English makes it clear that you are asking a question by an inverted sentence order and a change of intonation. 'You are my friend,' becomes, 'Are you my friend?' Chicheŵa doesn't usually change the sentence order when changing from a statement to a question. Questions are shown more by intonation (the rise and fall of tones) and 'question words' (like *what, where, why,* etc.).

Kodi

This word basically indicates that the sentence is a question. It is commonly put on the front of a question that doesn't have another question word (who, what, where) in the sentence. It is also optionally added on questions that do have another question word in them.

Kodi mulipo?   Are you around?
Kodi zimene zinachitika zinali zabwino?   Were the things that happened good?
Kodi moyo wanu ukuyenda bwino? Is your life going well?

'Kodi' can be at the end of the sentence instead of the beginning:
Moyo uli bwino kodi? Is life good?
Sakupezeka kodi?   Is he not around? (kupezeka – to be around, available)

'Kodi' can be used optionally in questions with other question words:
Kodi muli bwanji? How are you?

'Kodi' can be used alone as an expletive showing unbelief:
'Kodi?!' 'Really?!'

Bwanji

This word basically means 'how?'
Muli bwanji? How are you?
Izi zikutheka bwanji? How are these things possible?
(kutheka – to be possible)
Munayenda bwanji? How did you travel?
Bwana anapeza bwanji ndalama zimenezi? How did the
boss find this money?

Notice that it usually goes right after the verb.
Munthuyu anafika bwanji ku Zomba kuno? How did this
person arrive here in Zomba?

It's use can be much broader than 'how':
'Bwanji?' 'What's up? What's going on?'
'Munthuyu bwanji?' 'What about this person?'
'Simudziŵa Chicheŵa bwanji?' Why don't you know
Chicheŵa? (How is it possible?)

-a bwanji – How much?
Ndithiremo madzi a bwanji? How much water should I
pour in?
Bukhuli ndi la bwanji? How much (money) is this book?

To ask how much something costs:
Izi bwanji? What about these (zinthu)? (pointing)
Mukupanga bwanji tomato? How much are you charging
for the tomatoes? (Literally: You are making how

141

tomatoes?)
Tomato ali pa bwanji?   The tomatoes are how much?
(Literally: The tomatoes are on how?)
Nsapatozi ndi za bwanji?   How much are these shoes?

In very informal, colloquial Chicheŵa, 'bwanji?' is often said as 'bwa?'
Muli bwa? How are you?
Izi nza bwa? These (zinthu) are how much (of how)?

Chiyani

'Chiyani' means 'what?'   Make a habit of using it after the verb, but sometimes you'll hear it before the verb.
Ichi ndi chiyani? What is this?
Akupanga chiyani? What is he making?
Chinabwera chiyani? What came?
Chinabwera ndi chiyani? What came? (It came was what?)
Chingandithandize chiyani?   What can help me?
Chingandithandize ndi chiyani? What can help me? (It can help me is what?)

Ndani / Yani

'Ndani' means 'who?'   Like 'bwanji' and 'chiyani,' 'ndani' likes to come after the verb.
Anabwera ndani? Who came?
Walakwa ndani? Who is at fault (has done wrong)?
Wapambana ndani? Who has won?
Waluza ndani? Who has lost? ('kuluza' from 'to lose')
Adzandithandiza ndani? Who will help me?
Anafika pano ndani? Who came here?
Anandikonzera zabwinozi ndani? Who prepared these good things for me? (kukonza – to prepare/repair; kukonzera – to

prepare for)

It can sometimes come before the verb if the speaker so chooses:

Ndani adzatilekanitsa ndi chikondi cha Mulungu?

Who will separate us from the love of God?

(kuleka – to forsake; kulekana – to forsake one another; kulekanitsa – to separate; to make two parties leave each other)

Ndinam'thandiza ndani? Who did I help?

'Ndani' is actually a contraction of 'ndi yani'. This accounts for the fact that 'ndi' as a verb is always omitted before it.

Abwino ndani? Who are the good? (instead of 'Abwino ndi ndani?')

'Yani' is used less frequently:

Mwanayu ndi wa yani? Whose is this child?

Kuno ndi kwa yani? Whose is this place (who is the chief of this village)?

-tani

This very versatile question word is a verb meaning 'do what?' or 'say what?' In many ways it is used just like other verbs:

Pamenepo munatani? What did you do at that point?

Ndalama zitatha, tidzatani? When the money has finished, what will we do?

It takes a very important role in the verbal adjective form by indicating 'what kind':

Munthu wotani? What kind of person?

Zinthu zimene munapeza kumeneko zinali zotani? The
things that you found there were what kind of things?

'Motani' and 'kotani' can indicate 'how':
Anadwala motani? What was he sick of? or How sick was
he?
Mwanayo anam'nyamula motani? How did she pick up the
child? (roughly? gently?)
Anakalipira motani? How angry was he? What was his
anger like? (kukalipira – to get angry)
Mulungu ndi wokhulupirika kotani? How faithful is God?
(kukhulupirika – to be faithful; believable)

-ti

When this little word is used as a question, it takes the
verb prefixes (a-, zi-, chi-, u-, li-, etc.) and has the meaning
of 'which?' It presupposes that there are several things from
which to choose.
Nsomba yabwino ndi iti? Which is a good fish?
Chimanga chabwino ndi chiti? Which is the good maize?
Anthu aku Lilongwe ndi ati? Which are the people from
Lilongwe?

-ngati

'How much?' 'How many?' It also takes the prefixes
that normally go on the verb.
Akufuna ndalama zingati? How much money does he want?
Muli ndi nkhuku zingati? How many chickens do you
have?
Pasukulu pano pali ana angati? How many children are at
this school?
Alipo anthu angati pamudzi pa aKamwendo? How many

people are there at Chief Kamwendo's village?

Ndalama zingati?   How much money?
Nthochizi mukugulitsa ndalama zingati? You are selling
these bananas for how much money?

-nji

Usually, -nji takes the meaning of 'what kind?' and
sometimes 'what?'   It takes the prefixes that normally go
on an adjective. Zinthu zanji (what kind of things), anthu
anji (what kind of people), bukhu lanji, nsomba yanji, mavuto
anji, etc.

Anakupatsa nkhuku zanji? What kind of chickens did she
give you?
Ndi galimoto yanji? What kind of vehicle is it?
Mumagwira ntchito yanji? What kind of work do you do?
(kugwira ntchito – to work)

A very common construction using -nji employs the
word 'mtundu' (kind) for obvious reasons:
Mtengowu ndi wa mtundu wanji? What kind of tree is this?
Mitamboyi ndi ya mtundu wanji? What kind of clouds are
these?
Ndi za mtundu wanji nsaŵaŵazi? What kind of peas are
these? (nsaŵaŵa\nsaŵaŵa – peas)

Liti

'Liti' means 'when?' It really is just the form of '-ti'
above that accords with 'tsiku' (day).
Tsiku liti? Which day?
Liti? When?

Mudzabwera liti? What day will you come?
Kutchalitchi kwanu mumakumana liti ndi liti?   At your
church when do you meet? (literally: 'when and when')

For 'when?' in the sense of 'what time?' use 'Nthaŵi yanji?'
Ndifike kwanu nthaŵi yanji? What time should I come to
your place?
Compare with:
Ndifike kwanu liti?   *What day* should I come to your
place?

Ngati

'Ngati' normally means 'if'.   Sindidziŵa ngati
ndingabwere. I don't know if I can come. But it can be used
in a question sentence to indicate that the speaker expects the
answer of the question to be 'no.' The question is asked with
a tone of incredulity.
Anyamata amaphika ngati?   Do boys cook? As though
boys cook!
Mulungu anganame ngati?   God can't lie, can He?

Kaya

This word can be used to introduce questions with the
idea of 'and what about…'
Ndili bwino. Kaya inu? I am fine. What about you?
Kaya nkhuku, zili bwino? What about the chickens? Are
they fine?

Nanga

Similar to 'kaya' in its 'what about' usage.
Ndili bwino. Nanga inu?   I am fine, what about you?

146

Sometimes 'nanga' introduces a question to which you expect the answer is 'no'.
Nanga kukhala ku Bangwe n'kwabwino?   It's not good to stay in Bangwe, is it?

'Ngati' is stronger.
Kukhala ku Bangwe n'kwabwino ngati? It couldn't be good to stay in Bangwe!
'Nanga' and 'ngati' can be in the same question:
Nanga kukhala ku Bangwe n'kwabwino ngati?

Kodi anthu aja abwera?   Have those people come?
Mudzabwera maŵa kodi?   Will you come tomorrow?
Zimenezi bwanji?   What's up with these things?
Tingadziwe bwanji kuti ng'ombezi ndi zazikazi?   How can we know that these cows are female? (kuti – that)
Mapeyalaŵa mukugulitsa pa bwanji?   How much are you selling these avocadoes for?
Makinawo ndi a chiyani?   What are those machines for? (makina – machine)
Dzina lanu ndani?   What is your name?
Ameneyu ndi mwana wa ndani?   Whose child is this?
Ameneyu ndani?   Who is this?
Pamenepa titani?   What should we do now?
Kodi munagula kompyuta iti?   Which computer did you buy?
Ndikufuna mango. – Atiwo?   I want mangoes. – Which ones?
Mukufuna mango angati?   How many mangoes do you want?

Kodi bambo Phiri anagula galimoto yanji?   What kind of
car did Mr. Phiri buy?

Akuyenda bwanji malonda? How are sales going?

Nanga inu, mukuona bwanji?   What about you, how do you
see it? What is your opinion?

Chapter 26: The Verb Changers

There are several endings that go on verbs that actually become a part of the verb itself and change the meaning in some way. These are not just regular suffixes that are added on the end of the verb. Basically, we can say a new word is made when one of these is added.

-tsa

This ending makes a verb 'causative.'
kudya (to eat), kudyetsa (to feed)
kudala (to be blessed), kudalitsa (to bless)
kuyenda (to walk, go), kuyendetsa (to drive)
kufala (to spread, something spreading on its own, such as a disease), kufalitsa (to spread something)

This '-tsa' ending can also be used on some verbs to make them 'intensive' and then it's sometimes doubled:
kuona (to see), kuonetsetsa (to look hard, carefully)
kudziŵa (to know), kudziŵitsitsa (to know thoroughly)
kufuna (to want), kufunitsitsa (to desire strongly)
kukhala (to sit, stay), kukhalitsa (to stay for a long time)

Notice that when the '-tsa' ending is added to a verb, what used to be the final '-a' on the original verb changes to '-e-' or '-i-'.

> kugwir<u>a</u> – kugwir<u>i</u>tsa
> kuloŵ<u>a</u> – kuloŵ<u>e</u>tsa

Here are the rules on whether to change the '-a' to '-i-' or '-e-':

1. If the verb's **second to last vowel** is a, i, or u, replace the last '-a' with '-i-'.

> kufala > kufalitsa
>
> kugula (to buy) > kugulitsa (to sell)
>
> kupanga (to make, do) > kupangitsa (to make someone make or do something)
>
> kugwira ntchito (to work) > kugŵiritsa ntchito (to use)

All these words have a, u, or i as their second to last vowel, thus they change the final '-a' to '-i-'.

2. If the verb's **second to last vowel** is e or o, or if the word is a single syllable, replace the final '-a' with '-e-'.

> kubwera (to come) > kubweretsa (to bring)
>
> kuona (to see) > kuonetsa (to show)
>
> kutha (to finish, run out) > kuthetsa (to use up, cause to finish or end)

Some verbs lose their whole final syllable when '-tsa' is added.

> kutsika (go down) > kutsitsa (bring down)

Certain verbs have two '-tsa' forms, one that retains the original stem's last syllable and one that discards it.

> kubwera (to come) > kubweretsa (to bring)
>
> kubwera (to come) > kubwetsa (to bring)

Note: All the other 'Verb Changer' endings mentioned in this chapter (-ra, -za, -ka, -dwa) have the same rules for changing the last vowel to '-i-' or '-e-' before adding that particular ending.

-ra

This ending does several things. For most action verbs that can't normally be used with objects, the '-ra' ending enables the verb to be used with an object by giving it an 'applied' sense (to, for, etc.).

Kuthamanga. To run.
Kuthamangira. To run for, to, etc.
Kumuthamangira. To run to him.

Kugwa. To fall.
Kugwera. To fall on.
Ndinamugwera. I fell on him.

Kufa. To die.
Kufera. To die for.
Yesu anatifera ife chifukwa cha machimo athu. Jesus died for us because of our sins.

The -ra ending can shew some relational purpose or direction:
Kupatsa. To give.
Kupatsira. To leave something with someone for them to give to someone else.
Kuzimitsa nyale. To put out the light.
Kuzimitsira nyale. To put out the light till later.

kuonera	to observe	from kuona (to see)
kubwerera	to return	from kubwera (to come)
kuyendera	to visit	from kuyenda (to travel)
kuŵerengera	to reckon to the account of, from kuŵerenga
(to count/read)		

Special uses of the -ra ending:
1. The word 'm'mene' is often used to mean 'how' (as in, 'I saw how he was doing it.') in which case the verb that follows 'm'mene' always takes the -ra ending. If the verb already has a -ra ending, it takes a double -rera or -rira.
Ndaona m'mene amachitira. I have seen how he does (it).
M'mene ndikuonera, zinthuzi zili bwino. As (how) I see (it), these things are good.
Kumvera. To obey.
M'mene amandimverera, … The way he obeys me, …

2. The -ra ending is used with -po or -ko to mean 'a little, or a little more.'
Zikufunikirapo. They are a little (more) important.
John ndi wotalikirapo. John is a little taller. (kutalika – to be tall)

3. Followed by -tu the -ra ending can give the word two additional meanings:
a. 'Totally, completely'
    Kutha. To run out, be finished.
    Kutheratu. To be totally, completely finished.
    Mafuta atheratu. The oil/petrol is completely finished.
b. 'Beforehand, in anticipation'
    Kulima. To hoe, cultivate.
    John alimiratu. John has hoed his gardens early, before the rains.
    Kudzala. To plant.
    Anadzaliratu. He planted early.

-dwa

This ending indicates passive voice. For example, it takes the word 'to eat' and makes it 'to be eaten,' the word 'to find' and makes it 'to be found,' and so on.

kupha (to kill)	kuphedwa (to be killed)
kupatsa (to give)	kupatsidwa (to be given)

Katundu wagulidwa. The stuff has been bought. (katundu – things, luggage, stuff)
Ndasiyidwa. I have been left (alone).

-ka

-Ka also has a 'passive' meaning, like -dwa, but it more often gives the verb the idea of what I will call 'passive possibility.' It makes 'to buy' into 'to be cheap (to be able to be bought)' rather than 'to be bought' (as -dwa would do).

kugula (to buy)	kugulika (to be cheap)
kuona (to see)	kuoneka (to be visible)
kufuna (to want, need)	kufunika (to be important)
kupeza (to find)	kupezeka (to be available)
kuchita (to do)	kuchitika (to happen)

Some verbs actually do use this form instead of -dwa as regular passive:

kudziŵa (to know)	kudziŵika (to be known, famous)
kumva (to hear)	kumveka (to be heard, be audible)

Strangely enough, sometimes -ka acts like -tsa, making the verb causative or intensive:

kudwala (to be sick)	kudwalika (to be very sick)
kugona (to lie down)	kugoneka (to lay down)

Mayi wagoneka mwana. Mother has put the child down to sleep.

-za

This ending is similar to -tsa, but it is only used with certain words.

kutsogola (to go in front, lead)
kutsogoza (to make something go forward)
Notice how, with this example, the -za ending swallowed up what used to be the last syllable.
kubweza (to restore, return something, revenge) from kubwera (to come)
kubwereza (to repeat) from kubwera (to come)
kudzoza (to apply oil, lotion to someone else, anoint) from kudzola (to apply oil, lotion to oneself)

-na each other, one another

This item does not properly belong in this chapter because it is just an ordinary suffix. On the end of a verb it gives the idea of 'to one another'. Where 'kudziŵa' is to know, 'kudziŵana' is to know one another. 'Kumenya' is to hit or beat someone, but 'kumenyana' is to beat each other, in other words, to fight.

Note that it is merely glued on the end of the verb with no change whatsoever to the last syllable.

Tionana. We'll see each other.
Kuyenda. To walk.
Kuyendera. To visit.
Kuyenderana. To visit each other.

154

'Ndi' connects the verb witth -na to an object.
Ndinaonana ndi James.   I saw (each other with) James.
Galu wathu amamenyana ndi agalu ena onse. Our dog
fights with all other dogs.

Kukumana.   To meet.
Sindinakumane naye (ndi iye). I never met him.
Anakumana ndi amayi kutawuni. She met mother in town.
Tidzakumana ndi Mulungu pa tsiku lomaliza. We will meet
with God on the last day.

Chapter 27: Might, May, Can, Could, Even

Kukhoza

This verb can variably be translated, 'to be able,' 'to pass a test,' 'to excel,' or 'to succeed.' When used as, 'I can...', it often indicates 'situational' ability rather than physical competence. In other words, 'I can do such-and-such because I'm not busy, not hindered by circumstances, etc.'

I can go with you. Ndikhoza kupita nanu. (I am available to go with you.)

Akhoza kubwera mwezi wamaŵa. He can come next month.

Sakhoza kundithandiza chifukwa cha maliro. He is not able to help me because of a funeral.

Kutha

'Kutha' means 'to be able' but refers more to physical ability.

Sinditha kuona. I can't see. (I'm blind, or something is in the way.)

Atha kuyenda. He can walk. (He's not too old, or his broken leg healed.)

-nga-

This infix makes a verb mean 'can, or, might do'.

Sindingapite. I cannot go.

Angaone zodabwitsa. They might see amazing things.

Akuba angabwere usiku. Thieves could come at night.

Thus in certain constructions it takes the meaning of 'lest, in

156

case':

Osapita kumeneko, mungapeze zovuta. Don't go there, in case you find troubles.

Thaŵapo! Ungagwe. Get away from there! You might fall!

-ngathe

This is just the -nga- infix on the word 'kutha'. I have included it separately since it is a very common form.

Angathe kupita. He can go.

Zingathe kusweka. They (zinthu) can break. (kusweka-to break)

Kuyenera

This is actually a verb meaning 'to be worthy, must, should' and we already saw it under the section on 'commands.'

Ayenera kupita. He should go. He ought to go.

It can also be used to comment on the probability of events:

Chimanga chiyenera kuchita bwino chaka chino. The maize should do good this year [since the rains were good].

Mabuku ayenera afika kale ku positi. The books probably already arrived at the post office.

Ngakhale

This word is the '-nga-' form of 'kukhala' without any prefix. It can be used as it is to mean 'even' or 'although'.

Ndili bwino ngakhale ndikumva mutu. I am fine even though I have a headache (feel my head).

Angakhale

This word is similar to the last one, meaning 'even':

Angakhale abusa anafika. Even the pastors came.

Kutheka

The passive form of 'Kutha', 'Kutheka' means 'to be possible', or 'to work'. Often used in general sentences with 'zi-'.

Zimenezo sizitheka ayi!   Those things won't work/are impossible.

Zatheka?   Have the things worked?
E, zatheka.   Yes, they've worked.
Ayi, sizinatheke, akuti ndibwerenso maŵa.   No it didn't work, they say I should come back tomorrow.

Chapter 28: Irregular Adjectives

There are several important adjectives that are different from other adjectives in the way they connect to nouns. They use irregular prefix systems.

-kha (only, alone, by one's self)

With pronouns:
ine ndekha (I myself)	ife tokha (we ourselves)
iwe wekha (you yourself)	inu nokha (you yourselves)
iye yekha (he himself)	iwo okha (they themselves)

With nouns:
1 munthu yekha	anthu okha
(a person alone/only a person)	(only people)
2 munda wokha	minda yokha
(only garden)	(only gardens)
3 chimanga chokha	zoonadi zokha
(only maize)	(only true things)
4 mbuzi yokha	nkhanga zokha
(only goat)	(only guinea fowl, pl.)
5 lero lokha	maŵa okha
(only today)	(only tomorrow)
6 ufa wokha	mausiku okha
(only flour)	(only nights)
7 kamphaka kokha	tiagalu tokha
(only kitten)	(only dogs)
Ku	kupita kokha
	(only going)
Pa, ku, mu	pokha, kokha, mokha

Kunyumba ndinapeza anyamata okha.
I found only boys at the house.
Zinthu zimene zithandiza ndi izi zokha.
The things that will help are only these.
Anachita yekha.   He did it himself.
Pang'ono pokha.   Only a little.
Amamwa madzi okha.   He only drinks water.

Kokha is often used as an adverb:
Amaŵerenga kokha; salemba.   He only reads; he doesn't
write.

'By himself' or 'by itself'
Anakhala payekha.   He stayed by himself.
Anadya nsima payokha.   He ate nsima by itself.

The word is often doubled for emphasis:
Ndikuona mdima wokhawokha.   I just see darkness only.
(mdima – darkness)
Chaka chinochi alima chimanga chokhachokha.   This year
he has cultivated only maize.

'Pokhapokha' can mean 'except,' 'only if,' 'unless':
Sitingadziwe zavutoli pokhapokha atatiuza anthu.
We can't know about this problem unless we are told by
people.
Pokhapokha mutabwera kunoko ndi pamene mukhoza
kundipeza.   Only if you come here can you find me.

-nse (whole, all, completely)

ine ndense (my whole self, all of me)
iwe wense (your whole self)
iye yense (all of him/her)
ife tonse (all of us)
inu nonse (all of you)
iwo onse (all of them)

1 tiyi yense	ana onse
(all the tea)	(all the children)
2 mudzi wonse	midzi yonse
(all the village)	(all the villages)
3 chikwama chonse	zakudya zonse
(the whole bag, purse)	(all the foods)
4 nyama yonse	mphamvu zonse
(all the meat)	(all the strength)
5 denga lonse	maungu onse
(the whole roof)	(all the pumpkins)
6 umphawi wonse	maujeni onse
(all the poverty)	(all the such and such)
7 kabuku konse	tiana tonse
(the whole pamphlet)	(all the little children)
Ku	kuphunzira konse
	(the whole learning)
Pa, ku, mu	ponse, konse, monse

Mawindo onse asweka.   All the windows have been broken.
(kuswa – to shatter something; kusweka – to shatter, be broken)
Felix amaŵerenga nthaŵi zonse. Felix reads at all times.
Amaŵerenga mabukhu onse.   He reads all books.

Konsekonse and ponseponse mean 'everywhere':
Dzuwa limawala konsekonse. The sun shines everywhere.
Felix amawerenga ponseponse.   Felix reads everywhere.

-na (another, other, different, some, any, more)

(no unique personal pronoun forms)

1 munthu wina
(a certain/another person)
2 mseu wina
(another road)
3 chifukwa china
(another reason)
4 nyimbo ina
(some song)
5 tsidya lina
(the other side)
6 udzu wina
(more grass)
7 kamnyamata kena
(another little boy)
Ku

Pa, ku, mu

agalu ena
(some/other dogs)
miyezi ina
(some months)
zovuta zina
(more troubles)
mbabva zina
(other burglars)
madera ena
(other areas)
mauta ena
(other bows)
tinyimbo tina
(some little songs)
Kuthamanga kwina
(another [kind] of running)
pena, kwina, mwina

'A Certain, Some' (-na -ke)
This word can be used in the following way to indicate a
more general, 'a certain...'
munthu wina wake – a certain person
chinthu china chake – a certain thing
anthu ena ake – certain people

162

ulendo wina wake – some journey
majumbo ena ake – certain plastic bags
ndiwo zina zake – certain relishes

Kodi mwanyamula chiyani? What are you carrying?
Basi, ndi mabuku ena ake akusukulu. It's just some school books.
Kodi ndalama anakupatsani zija ndi zingati?   How much is that money she gave you?
Ndi masauzandi ena ake.   It is some thousands.

-ni-ni (real, authentic, actual)

(no unique personal pronoun forms)

1 bambo weniweni	amayi enieni
(the real father)	(the actual mothers)
2 msika weniweni	misonkhano yeniyeni
(a real market)	(real meetings)
3 chitukuko chenicheni	zomera zenizeni
(genuine development)	(actual plants; kumera – to
sprout; chomera – plant)	
4 njobvu yeniyeni	nzeru zenizeni
(a real elephant)	(real wisdom)
5 boma lenileni	masamba enieni
(real government)	(actual greens)
Ku	kusoŵa kwenikweni
	(to be really missing, lost)

Pa, ku, mu – penipeni, kwenikweni, mwenimweni

Pamwamba penipeni – at the very top
Si zoona kwenikweni.   It's not really true.

Akunena zenizeni. He's saying the truth/real things.

Demonstrative takes the last place:

The demonstrative (this and that) usually takes the last place after all other adjectives that modify a noun.

Munthu wabwinoyu. Not, Munthuyu wabwino.
This good person.
Mnyamata womenyana kwambiriyo. That boy that fights a lot.
Bukhu lomwe ndikulikonda kwambiri lija ndi *Nthondo*.
That book I really like is *Nthondo*.
Chinthu china chokhacho chili m'dengu. The only other thing is in the basket.

Uyu ndi mwana wanga weniweni, palibenso wina, alipo yekha.   This is my real child, there is no other, he's the only one.

Mwana wanga wina sakonda sukulu kwenikweni.
Another/a certain one of my children doesn't really like school.

Nthaŵi zina, amakonda kuyenda kutchire kukasaka nyama.
Sometimes he like to go walking in the bush to hunt animals.

Chapter 29: Every, any

We learned the word 'all, whole' above:
anthu onse – all the people
nkhani yonse – the whole story, etc.

Aliyense
This same -nse word can be used to indicate 'any' or 'every,'
but it takes the word -li on the front:

mwana aliyense   (any/every child)
mpando uliwonse   (any/every chair)
chifukwa chilichonse (any/every reason)
mbabva iliyonse   (any/every thief)
khola lililonse   (any/every animal pen)
ufumu uliwonse   (any/every kingdom)
kagalu kalikonse   (any/every puppy)
kumalo kulikonse   (at any/every place)
pamalo paliponse   (on any/every place)
m'madzi mulimonse   (in any/all water)

Kulikonse, paliponse, and mulimonse are often used for
anywhere/everywhere.
Amangolowᴡa mulimonse. He just goes in anywhere.
Amayenda paliponse. He walks everywhere.
Kulikonse kumene amafika kunali mavuto. Everywhere/
anywhere where he would arrive, there would be troubles.

Aliyense just by itself means anyone, everyone, referring, of
course, to 'munthu'.
Aliyense abwere kwa Yesu. Everyone should come to Jesus.

Chilichonse by itself means anything, everything, referring

to 'chinthu'.
Ndikufuna chilichonse. I want anything.

Wina aliyense
Often the word -na (wina, china, zina, lina, ena, etc.) comes
between the noun and the word 'every,' without adding
much to the meaning.
Bwana wina aliyense. Any, every boss.
Zikwama zina zilizonse. Any, all purses, travelling bags.
Mau ena alionse. Any, all words.
Sukulu ina iliyonse. Any, every school

Sindinapeze ndalama ina iliyonse m'thumbamo.
I didn't find any money in that pocket.

Ndikufuna munthu wina aliyense amene angandithandize.
I want any person who can help me.

Mau a Mulunguŵa ndi a kwa munthu aliyense.
These words of God are for every person.

Katundu ameneyu mudzamuika pena paliponse pakhonde
paja.   This stuff you will just put anywhere on the porch
there.   (khonde\makonde – porch)

Ameneyu amangolima mwina mulimonse, chifukwa chake,
chimanga chake sichinabereke bwino. Sanapeze zokolola
zina zili zonse. This guy just cultivates anyhow, that's
why his maize didn't bear well. He didn't find any harvest
(things of harvest). (kukolola – to harvest)

166

Chapter 30: Adverbs

Adverbs are words that modify verbs, adjectives, or other adverbs. In English, examples of adverbs include:

I walk *quickly*. I swim *well*. They *hardly* want it.

In Chicheŵa, we find adverbs expressed by suffixes, infixes, and separate words.

Adverb Suffixes and Infixes

-di   **really, for sure**

Adzapitadi. He will really go.

Can be used with most verb forms, phrases and whole sentences.

Anabweradi. He really came.

Mulungu alipodi. God really is there.

Zoona! Truly!

Zoonadi! Truly! (stronger)

-tu   **surely, already, adds urgency to commands**

Pitanitu! Please go!

Ali bwinotu. He is really fine.

Ndakuuzanitu. I have told you already.

Tamveranitu! Listen to me! (kumvera – to listen, obey)

Ndalama zatheratu.

-ratu   **beforehand, completely**

Ndalama zatheratu. The money is completely finished.

Ndinadziŵiratu. I knew before (it happened).

Mphunzitsi anaiwaliratu. The teacher completely forgot. (kuiwala – to forget)

-nso   **again, also, as well**

Used with verbs, nouns, phrases.

Mpunganso ukufunika. Rice is also needed. (kufunika – to be important, needed)

Thoko akupitanso. Thoko is going again.

Ifenso, tikufuna buku. We also would like a book.

Titapita ku tawuni, tidzapitanso ku sukulu. After we go to town, we will also go to the school.

-be   **still (repetition or continuance of action)**

Ndimapempherabe. I still pray. (I haven't stopped.)

Zidzachitikabe chaka cha maŵa. They (zinthu) will still happen next year.

Sanabwerebe. He still hasn't come.

Kodi John wabwera? Ayi, koma abwerabe. Has John come. No, but he will still come.

-ngo-   **just, only**

Ndimangofuna kukuthandizani. I just wanted to help you.

Ndidzangobwera. I will just come (maybe without letting you know).

Zikungochitika. They are just happening (without an explanation).

Nkhuku zanga zimangofa. My chickens just die.

-ko, -po (ever, at all)

Sindinaonepo mzungu. I never saw a white man.

Ndinaphunzirako umekaniki. I did (at one point) study (car) mechanics.

-ko, -po (a little, a little more)

Aliko bwino. Ali bwinoko. He is a little better.

Akuchitapo bwino. He is a little well off.
Akuyeserapo. He is trying (at least a little).
Zinthu zolimbirapo… Things that are a little harder…

-ko, -po, -mo (there)
Anapitako chaka chatha. He went there last year.
Ndidzakapezako chimanga. I will go find maize there.

Single Word Adverbs

ndithu – truly, for sure
Ndidzabwera ndithu. I will come for sure.
As an exclamation:
Ndithu! For sure!
Ndithudi! Absolutely!

bwino – well, good, carefully, soon
Yendani bwino. Travel well.
Amaŵerenga bwino. He reads well.
Abwera bwino lomwe. He will come soon.

As an exclamation, 'Careful!'
Bwinotu! Ugwa! Careful, you'll fall!
Bwino bambo, musapite kumeneko! Careful, sir, you
shouldn't go there!

msanga – quickly, fast
Akubwera msanga. He is coming quickly.
Madzi akutuluka msanga. Water is coming out fast.
msangamsanga – very fast
Anadutsa msangamsanga. He passed by very quickly.

chabe – only
Anamwa madzi chabe. He only drank water.
Can be used with the infix -ngo- which can also mean 'just'/ 'only'.
Anangomwa madzi chabe. He only drank water.
Anali ndi mwana m'modzi (one) chabe. He had only one child.

Note: just like 'bwino', 'chabe' can be used as an adjective, where it means, 'worthless, bad':
Makoswe ndi achabe. Rats are worthless, bad. (khoswe\ makoswe – rat)
Anyamata achabe anandipeza pamsewu, ndi kundimenya kwambiri. Bad boys found me on the road and beat me up.
chabechabe – makes the meaning of 'worthless' stronger
Zinthuzi ndi zachabechabe. These things are utterly worthless.
pachabe – in vain
Usataye nthaŵi pachabe. Don't waste time.
(kutaya – to lose, throw away)

wamba – without special thought or care, anyhow, commonly; as an adjective, normal, ordinary
Zinthuzi sizipezeka wamba. These things aren't found commonly.
Bukhuli simungaliŵerenge wamba. This book you can't just read anyhow.

Note: Just like 'bwino' this word can be an adjective, but there is one interesting thing to remember, 'wamba' often takes no prefix.
John si munthu wamba. John is not an ordinary person.

170

Anthu wamba sangafike pano. Ordinary people can't come here.

makamaka – especially, probably
Nkhuku zimavuta, koma makamaka nkhanga. Chickens are troublesome, but especially guineafowl.
Makamaka mvula sichedwa. Probably the rain won't take long (in coming).

Verbs used as Adverbs
To make a verb into an adverb, usually use the prefix po-, ko-, or mo-.
posachedwa – soon, quickly (not being late)
Adzabwera posachedwa. He will come soon.
mosachedwa – soon, quickly (same as above)
Ndinafika mosachedwa. I arrived quickly.
posachedwapa – lately, not long ago
Zinatuluka posachedwapa. They (zinthu) came out lately.
mochedwa – slowly, late
Mvula inafika mochedwa. The rain came late. Also:
Inachedwa kufika. It was late in coming.
mofulumira – quickly, early
Makasuŵa amaonongeka mofulumira. These hoes are ruined quickly, soon.
Makasuŵa amafulumira kuonongeka. These hoes hurry to be ruined.
(kuononga – to destroy, ruin; kuonongeka – to be ruined, destroyed)

mo- is the most widely used in making adverbs from verbs
Anayendetsa njinga mothamanga kwambiri. He drove his bike very fast.

Anapanga zimenezo mosaganiza bwino. He did those things carelessly/without thinking well.

Zinachitika mosadziŵika bwino.   They (zinthu) happened in a way that is hard to understand. (kudziŵika – to be known, understandable)

Anagona movutikira. She slept fitfully. (kuvutikira – to be troubled)

mo- can also indicate 'while':
Anadya moyenda. He ate while walking.

Adverbs from Adjectives or Nouns:

mwa-

The mwa- adjective form is often used to form adverbs from adjectives or nouns.

mwachisaŵaŵa – disorderly, by chance, without proper preparation or consideration ('chisaŵaŵa' means 'disorder')
Musagulitse galimoto yanu mwachisaŵaŵa. Don't sell your vehicle without proper consideration.
Kudula mitengo mwachisaŵaŵa sibwino. Cutting down trees in a disorderly, unplanned fashion is not good.
Akuyenda mwachisaŵaŵa.   He is walking without purpose, just anyhow.

mwaulesi – lazily ('ulesi' means 'laziness')
Anagwira ntchito mwaulesi. They worked lazily.

mwangwiro – perfectly ('ngwiro' is an adjective meaning 'perfect, right')
Kumwamba tidzalemekeza Mulungu mwangwiro. In heaven we will honor God perfectly.

172

mwaluso – skillfully (luso – skill)
Akugwira ntchito mwaluso. He is working skillfully.

kwa-

The kwa- form is also used with certain words.
kwambiri – much, very
Amandikonda kwambiri. He loves me very much.
Zikomo kwambiri. Thank you very much.
Ali bwino kwambiri. He is very fine.
Ndalama zachepa kwambiri. (kuchepa – to be few, small)
There is a very small amount of money.

pa-

For pa- there are a few adverb forms.
pang'ono – a little
Ndikudziŵa Chicheŵa pang'ono.   I know Chicheŵa a little bit.
Akudwala pang'ono. He is a little sick.
Ng'ombe zimafanana ndi nkhumba pang'ono. Cows are a little similar to pigs. (kufanana – to be like, similar)
pang'onopang'ono – bit by bit, slowly, a little bit
Agogo amayenda pang'onopang'ono.   Grandfather walks slowly. (gogo\agogo – grandparent)
Madzi akuphwa pang'onopang'ono. The water is going down slowly. (kuphwa – to dry up of a liquid)
Ndikuphunzira Chicheŵa pang'onopang'ono. I am slowly learning Chicheŵa.
patalipatali – seldom
KuMangochi ndimapita patalipatali. I seldom go to Mangochi.
pafupipafupi – often
Tinkaonana nawo pafupipafupi.   We used to meet with them

regularly/often.

apo ndi apo – seldom, irregularly, a little
Si bwino kuŵerenga apo ndi apo.   It's not good to study/
read irregularly/seldom.

**choncho – like that, so, such (short form of
'chomwecho')**
Ndinamuona akupanga choncho.   I saw him doing so.
Momwe ndipangira, nanunso mupange choncho.   As I do,
you also should do the same.
Sindikonda njinga zachoncho.   I don't like bicycles like that.

chonchi – like this (short form of 'chomwechi')
Wina akapanga chonchi mundidziŵitse.   If someone does
like this you should tell me.   (kudziŵitsa – to tell, let one
know)
Buledi wachonchi ndi wachabe.   This kind of bread is
worthless.

Jemusi anangoyenda pang'onopang'ono popita kuchipatala.
James just walked little by little while going to the hospital.

Ine ndinamuonadi akuyenda choncho.
I really saw him walking like that.

Tinakambirana naye mwa chikondi koma anatiyankha
mokalipira.
We discussed with him lovingly but he answered us angrily.
(kukambirana – to discuss) (chikondi – love) (kuyankha – to
answer) (kukalipira – to be angry)

174

Anandimenya ndithu apa, choncho pakupweteka koopsya.
He hit me hard right here, thus it hurts badly/terribly.
(kuopsya – to be dangerous, terrible)

Bwino, mwanawe! Thaŵa galimoto!
Careful, you child! Get out of the way of the car!
(mwanawe – contraction of 'mwana iwe') (kuthaŵa – to run
away from)

Zamalirozo anamufotokozera bwinobwino.
Those issues concerning the funeral he explained carefully
to her. (maliro – funeral) (kufotokozera – to explain to)

Kuphiri kuja musamangokwera wamba; mungagwetu!
Don't just climb the mountain anyhow; you could really
fall!

Chapter 31: Comparative and Superlative

In English, we use the words 'more' and 'most' or the suffixes '-er' and '-est' to compare things with each other.

John is the smartest boy in the village.
This tree is taller than that one.
This is the most wonderful place I have ever been.
John is more diligent than the other farmer.

Comparisons in Chicheŵa are shown in several different ways. There are no direct correspondants to the English words 'more' and 'most'.

1. 'Kuposa' is a word meaning to 'do more or be more'. 'Kupambana' is a word that means to 'win, do best, or go beyond.'

With these two words, many 'more' and 'most' sentences can be built.

Nyumbayi ndi yabwino koposa iyo. (note ko- adverbial form)
This house is better than that one.

Nyumbayi ndi yabwino kopambana. This house is better/ best.

2. 'Kusiyana' is a word that means 'to be different.'

It is used to show 'more' or 'most' by signifying 'rather than/as opposed to'.

Nyumbayi ndi yabwino kusiyana ndi iyo.
This house is good rather/as opposed to that one.

176

3. Other constructions are also helpful:

Mwa nyumba zonsezi, yabwino ndi iyi.
Out of all these houses, the good one is this one.

Pakati panyumba zonse, yabwino ndi iyi.
Among all the houses, the good one is this one.

Tikaonetsetsa nyumba zonse, yabwino ndi iyi.
(kuonetsetsa – intensive of 'look')
If we look carefully at all the houses, the good one is this one.

To say, 'John is the best student in his school,' we could say any of the following:

Yohane aposa ophunzira ena onse kusukulu.
John is better than all the other students at school.

Yohane apambana kwambiri kusiyana ndi ena onse kusukulu.
John has excelled much more/as opposed to all the others at school.

Kunena za ophunzira akusukuluyi, Yohane ndi amene akhoza kwambiri.
Speaking of students at this school, John is the one who has excelled most. (kukhoza – to excel, to win)

4. Sometimes a -po or -ko ending is put on a verb to make it comparative (it seems to indicate 'a little better', 'a little more', etc.).

Yohane amachitako bwino pamaphunziro.
John does somehow better on his studies.

Anthu ochitako bwino palibe pano.
There aren't any well-off/richer people here.

Sometimes the -ra ending goes before the -po or -ko:

Buku ili ndi lofunikirapo kusiyana ndi ena aja.
This book is more important than (as opposed to) those others.

Tomatoyu ndi wodulirapo. (kudula – to be expensive)
These tomatoes are more expensive.

Izi ndi zolimbirapo. (kulimba – to be hard)
These are a little harder.

Masamu anaphwekerapo. (kuphweka – to be easy) Math was a little easier.

5. Often comparative and superlative ideas are shown by making 'universal' statements with the normal form of the adjective, without any qualifying words at all.

Phiri lalikulu ku Malaŵi ndi Mulanje.
The tallest mountain in Malaŵi is Mulanje.
Mpingo waukulu ku Italy ndi wachikatolika.   The biggest church/denomination in Italy is Catholic.

❖❖❖

Madzi aku Zomba ndi abwino koposa ena onse aku Malaŵi kuno.
The water in Zomba is better than all the other water here in Malaŵi.

Madzi aku Blantyre ndi abwinoko kusiyana ndi madzi aku Mangochi.
The water in Blantyre is a little better than the water in Mangochi.

Madzi aku Mangochi ndi abwino, koma madzi aku Zomba ndi abwino kwambiri.
The water in Mangochi is good but the water in Zomba is better.

Munthu wamkulu kwambiri kuno ndi agogo athuŵa.
The greatest/oldest person here is this our grandparent.

Kodi Misozi ali bwanji? How is Misozi?
Akuchitirako bwino kusiyana ndi dzulo.
She's doing a little better than yesterday.

Christopher ndi wonenepa kwambiri, koma bambo wake ayi. Christopher is very fat, whereas his father is not.

Ntchitoyi ndi yapafupi kwambiri, iyo ndi yapatali.
This job is very easy, that one is hard. (ie. This job is easier than that one.)
(-apafupi – easy; -apatali – hard)

Chapter 32: Conjunctions

These are words that join other words or phrases together, like English *and, but, or, for,* etc.

ndí – and, with, by

Note that when used as a conjunction, 'ndí' is pronounced with a high tone. The being verb 'ndi' carries a low tone.

and: Tinapita ndi kubwera.   John ndi Alefa akubwera.
We went and came. John and Alefa are coming.

with: Tidzabwera ndi abambo. We will come with father.

by: Zinatengedwa ndi mkango. They (nkhuku) were taken by a lion.

Contractions are very common when 'ndi' is used to mean 'with':

Anapita nawo (ndi iwo).   He went with them.
Mpunga nawonso (ndi uwonso) ndi wofunika. Rice also is important.
Thoko nayenso (ndi iyenso) akupita. Thoko also is going.
Tidzaonana naye.   We will see him. (see each other with him).
Anakumana nazo.   He met with them (zinthu).
('Kukumana nazo,' means, 'to experience real trouble'.)

When a sentence has a series of two or more verbs, the connecting 'and' often merges with the verb prefix for a simple 'na-' on the front of the verb.

Ndinaona galu nayamba kuthaŵa. I saw a dog and started to run away.

Adzapita ku Lilongwe nadzaona Wolemekezeka Martin Phiri. He will go to Lilongwe and see the Honorable Martin Phiri.

(kulemekeza – to honor; kulemekezeka – to be honored, honorable)

ndipo – and

(joining independent clauses or sentences)
Tinapita ku Blantyre, ndipo iwo anapita ku Thyolo. We went to Blantyre and they went to Thyolo.

koma – but

I tried hard, but I have failed. Ndinayesetsa, koma ndalephera.

(kuyesetsa – intensive of kuyesa 'to try')

komabe – but still, even

Anavulala, komabe ali bwino. He was wounded (kuvulala) but he's still alright.

Nyama yankhuku imakoma kwambiri, komabe yankhanga nayonso ili bwino. Chicken meat tastes best, but even guinea fowl is good as well. (nkhanga – guinea fowl)

komanso – and also

Tinapeza anyamata atatu pa mseu: Jemusi, Hastings, komanso Rubeni. We found three boys on the road: Jemusi, Hastings, and also Rubeni.

komatu – but
(the -tu ending might make it a little more emphatic)
Nkhanga ili bwino, eee, komatu nkhuku! Yes, guinea fowl
is good, but really chicken (is better)!

kapena – or
(and maybe, whether, either...or)
Kodi mukufuna ndalama kapena chakudya? Do you want
money or food?
Amafuna apite maŵa kapena mkucha. He wants to go
tomorrow or the next day.

Either this or that. Kapena ichi kapena icho.
Whether I live or die, I will still praise the Lord. Kapena
ndikhala moyo kapena ndifa, ndilemekezabe Ambuye.
(Note: for the last sentence 'kaya' could be used just as
well: 'Kaya ndikhala moyo kaya ndifa...)
Maybe I will come tomorrow. Kapena ndidzabwera maŵa.

mwina – maybe, somehow, somewhere
(literally from 'm'njira mwina,' 'm'malo mwina', etc.)
Mwina kukhala ndi mabukhu ambiri si bwino. Maybe to
have a lot of books is not good.   -or- Somehow/sometimes
to have a lot of books is not good.
Mwina kumudzi sikumapezeka anthu achifundo chotere.
Maybe/sometimes in the village there aren't (found) people
this merciful. (chifundo – mercy, kindness)

mwina mwake – maybe, somehow, somewhere, etc.
Mwina mwake sakupeza bwino. Maybe he's not feeling
good.
Anangoloŵera mwina mwake. He just went in somewhere.

182

(kuloŵera – applied form of kuloŵa, to go in, to enter)

tsopano – now, then
Tsopano, John atafika paja, zomuchitikira zinali motere…
Now when John had gotten there, what happened to him
was like this…

'Tsopano' can be shortened to 'tsono.'
Tsono, titani nanga? Now, what do we do?

mpaka, mpakana – until
Mudzagwira ntchito kuno mpaka liti? You'll work here
until when?
Ndinasungidwa ndi agogo anga mpakana chaka cha 2001. I
was taken care of by my grandparent until the year 2001.
(kusunga – to keep; kusungidwa – to be kept)

kufikira – until
…kufikira liti? …until when?
Mwapenta mpandawu kufikira pati? How far have you
gotten on painting this fence?
kuyambira … kufikira – from … to
Ndinagwira kuja kuyambira chaka cha 1998 kufikira cha
2003. I worked there from the year of 1998 to that of 2003.

kuyambira … mpaka – from … until
Mayi Phiri anadwala kuyambira Juni mpaka Disembala.
Mrs. Phiri was sick from June to December.
Mbiri yamunthu ameneyu ikukambidwa m'madera onse
kuyambira ku Blantyre mpakana ku Machinga. The story
of this person is being discussed in all the areas from
Blantyre to Machinga. (mbiri – story, history; dera\madera

– area; kukamba – to talk about, discuss)

kuchokera ... mpaka – from ... until
Kuchokera pomwe pali mtengo wamangopo mpakana pano tizilima ponsepa. From where there is the mango tree over there up to here we should hoe the whole place.

choncho (contraction of chomwe'cho) – so, like that
Timayenda choncho. We travel like that.
Lero ndi Khirisimasi, choncho anthu onse abizinesi sakugwira ntchito. Today is Christmas, so all business people aren't working.

chonchi (contraction of chomwe'chi) – so, like this
Apa, timapanga chonchi. At this point, we do like this.
Anandiona ndikukhala chonchi. He saw me sitting like this.

kuti – that
Ndifuna kukuuzani kuti . . .   I want to tell you that . . .

chifukwa chake – therefore
Chifukwa chake, pangani zimenezi. Therefore, do these things.

Amosi ndi ine timakonda kukaŵedza nsomba.
(kuŵedza – to fish)
Amos and I like to go fishing.
Amosi amakonda kukaŵedza nsomba pamodzi ndi ine.
Amos likes to go fishing together with me.
(pamodzi – together)

184

Amosi anathandizidwa ndi ine.
Amos was helped by me.
Ndalama zachepa, nazonso za Amos zachepa kwambiri.
The money is too little, even as for (with) that of Amos, it is too little.
Anakaonana naye. He went and met with him.
Madzi anasefukira, ndipo anthu anayamba kuthaŵa.
The water overfloẇed, and the people began to run away.
Anthu anathaŵa, koma ena anafa.
The people ran away, but some died.
Nthochi sindikufuna, koma mandimu.
(nthochi\nthochi – bananas; lindimu\mandimu – lemon)
I don't want bananas, but lemons.
Ena a ife tikudwala chifuwa, komabe tili bwino.
(chifuwa\zifuwa – chest, cough)
Some of us are sick with a cough, but still we are OK.
Mwina mwake chitsimechi chidzakhala zaka.
Maybe this well will be around for years.
Kapena ana athu nawo adzamwa madzi ameneŵa.
Maybe our children as well (nawo – with them/even them) will drink this water.
Ndinakhala m'nyumba muja kuyambira mwezi wa Meyi mpaka wa Juni.   I stayed in that house from the month of May to June.
Kuyambira pano kufikira nditafa, sindidzapitanso kumenekujako.   From now till I die, I won't go again to that place (the one I already mentioned).
Ngati mukufuna kuphika nkhuku, pangani chonchi.   If you want to cook chicken, do like this.
Choncho, tafika kumapeto amsonkhano wathu.
Thus we have come to the end of our meeting.
(mapeto – end; msonkhano\misonkhano – meeting)

Ndikufuna kuti mudzatchetche kuyambira pampanda pano mpaka pamiyala apo. I want you to slash from the fence here up to the rocks there.
(kutchetcha – to slash, cut grass; mwala\miyala – rock; mpanda\mipanda – fence)

Chapter 33: Ideophones

Ideophones form a very important group of words in Chicheŵa. These are 'sound words.' They give a mental sound picture of what the speaker is talking about.

Look at these examples:
Dengu linadzadza see!   The basket filled up all the way. (kudzadza – to fill up)
Anaima nji!   He stood firm. (kuima – to stand)
Mitambo inada bii!   The clouds were black. (kuda – to be dark)

The ideophones above ('see,' 'nji,' 'bii') are all used as adverbs, adding color to the verb in the sentence. But ideophones can be used for different parts of speech.

-ti and ideophones:
The verb -ti (to say) is very commonly used with ideophones with the -ngo- infix.
Ine ndinangoti phee!   I just was quiet! I just said, 'Phee!'
Mtsinje unangoti waa. The river roared. The river just said, 'Waa.'
Chitseko chikangoti kho! Udziŵa kuti ameneuja wafika. When the door slams, you'll know that that person has arrived. When the door says, 'Kho!' You'll know...

Some ideophones to learn:
Basi!   end, finished, all the way
Basi, siyani!   That's all, stop!
Ndili bwino basi. I'm just OK.
Amayi okha basi. Only women.

Chinthu chimodzi basi. Only one thing.
Kwabasi. Too much, very much, etc.
Ndinachifuna kwabasi. I wanted it a lot.

Bii!   black
Mitambo yabii!   (tone drops on 'bii') Black clouds.

Phee!   quiet, not talking
Bile angoti phee!   Billy is just quiet.

Chete!   quiet, calm
Mwana azikhala chete.   A child should be quiet.

Mbe!   bright, white
Mitambo inali mbe!   The clouds were bright.

Gogogo!   knocking
Jemusi anangoti gogogo!   James knocked.
(related to kugogoda – to knock)

Dzidzidzi   suddenly
Nkhuku inatuluka mwadzidzidzi. The chicken suddenly
came out.

Tchutchutchu   frankly, honestly
Anandiuza mwatchutchutchu. He told me the whole truth.

Lowu!   entering (from kuloŵa)
Anangoti lowu.   He just came in.

Myaa!   smooth

188

Pha!   sudden arrival
Munthu anangobwera pha!   Someone just came.

Zii!   no one home, tasteless, cool, insipid,
boring, quiet, not talking
Kunyumba kuli zii. At home there's no one there.
Ndiwo ya zii. Tasteless soup.
Nkhani ya zii. Boring story.
Nditamufunsa za nkhani ija, anangoti zii, osayankha.
When I asked hime about that issue, he just was quiet, not
answering. (nkhani – story, subject, issue, news)

Gwa!   hard, tough, tough-looking
Mwala wa gwa!   Hard rock.

Yuu!   staring
Ana onse anangoti yuu!   All the children just stared.

Balamanthu!   appear suddenly
Asifa anangoti balamanthu pakhomo!   Asifa just appeared
at the door!

Kalikiliki   busy
Dalo ali kalikiliki kudziŵitsa anthu zotsatira zachisankho.
Dalo is busy informing people of the election results.
(kudziŵitsa – causative of kudziŵa; chisankho – election,
vote, choice)

Ogo!   Disappointment, loss
Ogo, ndataya foni!   Oh no, I've lost my phone!

Chapter 34: Mnzanga, Mphwanga, and Manga

Mnzanga is often translated as my friend, companion, or fellow. When it follows a noun as in 'mphunzitsi mnzanga', it means, 'my fellow teacher.' Its end changes according to which possessive pronoun it refers to (my friend, his friend, etc.)

Mnzanga (my friend)   Mnzathu (our friend)
Mnzako (your (s) friend)   Mnzanu (your (pl) friend)
Mnzake (his, her friend)   Mnzawo (their friend)

Anzanga (my friends)   Anzathu (our friends)
Anzako (your (s) friends)   Anzanu (your (pl) friends)
Anzake (his friends)   Anzawo (their friends)

This word doesn't always mean 'friend,' although it is often used that way. It more properly means 'companion' or 'fellow.' Where you want to indicate actual friendship, 'bwenzi' is more clear. 'Mnzanga' refers to someone who shares something in common with the one speaking.
Mnzanga – my friend, companion, associate
Mnzanga wadzina – namesake
Mnzanga wazaka – agemate
Mnzanga wakusukulu – schoolmate
Mnzanga wakuntchito – workmate
Mbusa mnzanga – my fellow pastor
Mzungu mnzanga – my fellow European

Mnzanga not only can change in its end, but also in its prefix 'm-'.
190

It can take any class prefix to mean a 'fellow thing'.
Chinthu chinzake – its fellow thing
Nkhuku zinzake – its fellow chickens
Nkhuku zinzawo – their fellow chickens
Dzuwa lilibe linzake. The sun has no 'fellow'. (It is only one, that is, incomparable.)
Mulungu alibe mnzake. God has no equal, fellow.
Munthu wopanda mnzake. An uncomparable person (without an 'equal'), or lonely person (without a 'friend').

This word is often translated into English as 'other' or 'the other one.'
Chinthu chokhudzana ndi chinzake. Something that touches another.
Nyumbayi ndi yaikulu koposa inzake. This house is bigger than the other one.

There are two other words that act in a similar way to mnzanga, as far as the word endings go. These are mpwanga and manga.

Mpwanga – my younger sibling, relative (sometimes used as a friendly, though slightly patronizing name for someone who is not one's relative)
Mphwako – your (s) younger sibling, relative
Mphwanu – your (pl) ...
Mphwake – his/her/its ...
Mphwawo – their ...

Aphwanga – my younger siblings, relatives
Aphwako – your (s) ...
Aphwanu – your (pl) ...

Aphwake – his/her/its ...
Aphwawo – their ...

Manga – my mother
Mako – your (s) mother
Make – his/her/its mother

Amako – your (s) mother
Amake – his/her/its mother

Women are often known by the names of their children, 'the
mother of John,' 'the mother of Beatrice,' etc.
Make Joyce – the mother of Joyce
Make wa Joyce – the mother of Joyce
Amake a Joyce – the mother of Joyce (respectful)

Tabwera kuno, mphwanga! Come here, my 'younger
brother'.
Amayi anapita ku Chitipa ndi amake aBeatrice ndi amake
aPrecious. Mother went to Chitipa with the mother of
Beatrice and the mother of Precious.
Ndinakaona mnzanga kuchipatala. I went to see my friend
at the hospital.
Mtengo uwu wasiyana ndi inzake ili apayi. This tree is
different from the other trees that are over here.
Nyumba izizi ndi zolimba kusiyana ndi zinzawo mwakuti
tinazimanga ndi njerwa zabwino koposa.   These houses
are stronger than the other houses in that we built them with
better bricks.
Aŵa ndi anzanga a ku ntchito. These are my workmates.

Chapter 35: M-, Chi-, and U – Noun Prefixes

I haven't really talked a lot about 'noun prefixes' as a separate entity because for most of the classes they are the same as the verb prefix. 'M-' is known as the 'noun prefix' for the Mu-A Class. It can be helpful to note the uses of 'm-' as an indicator of a 'person', when it is used on various word 'stems' or 'roots':

-chewâ   >   Mchewâ (Chewâ person)
-khristu (Christ)   >   Mkhristu (Christian)
-silamu   >   Msilamu (Muslim)
-filika (stem from 'Africa') > Mfilika (African)
-kulu (big, large)   > mkulu (elder, important person)
-kazi (female)   >   mkazi (woman)
-kwati (kukwatira – to marry) > mkwati (bridegroom)

Of course, for plural, the 'm-' changes to 'a-' as you would expect:
Achewâ (Chewâ people), Akhristu (Christians), Asilamu (Muslims), Afilika (Africans), akulu (elders)

If 'chi-' takes the place of 'm-' in front of the stem, it can mean 'language/habits of…'
-chewâ   >   Chichewâ (Chewâ language)
-khristu ('Christ')   >   Chikhristu (Christianity)
wakuda (dark skinned person) > wachikuda (person with habits/customs of Africa)
-kazi (stem 'female') >   -chikazi (female, having to do with women), zovala zachikazi – women's clothes
mwana (child)   >   chibwana (childishness,

foolishness)

-kwati (from 'kukwatira') > chikwati (wedding)

m'bale (relative)　　>　chibale (relationship)

mzungu (European)　>　chizungu (language or habits of Europeans)

Now for 'u'! When 'u' goes on the front of a noun or stem, it gives an abstract meaning to the word.

moyo (life)　　　　>　umoyo (lifestyle)

bwino (good)　　　>　ubwino (goodness)

chitsiru (fool)　　　>　utsiru (foolishness)

-modzi (one)　　　>　umodzi (unity)

-tatu (three)　　　>　utatu (trinity)

-kulu (large, big)　>　ukulu (size)

mthenga (messenger) >　uthenga (message)

mtumiki (minister)　>　utumiki (ministry)

mkwati (bridegroom) >　ukwati (marriage, wedding, basically interchangeable with 'chikwati' above)

m'misiri (skilled labourer) > umisiri (skilled working)

mlendo (stranger, traveller) > ulendo (journey)

bwenzi (friend)　　>　ubwenzi (friendship)

mboni (person who bears witness) > umboni (testimony, witness)

m'bale (relative)　　>　ubale (relationship)

mfulu (a free person) >　ufulu (freedom)

Some other 'abstract' words that also start with 'u':

ukhondo (cleanliness)

usiŵa (poverty, unkemptness)

More on Noun Prefix Chi-

Chi- is sometimes also used as a prefix that makes things 'big'. When 'chi' is put on the front of an ordinary noun, the noun now has an added meaning of 'a big …'

Chinyumba – a mansion

Chikhasu – a huge hoe

Of course, now that the noun starts with 'chi-' it goes in the Chi-Zi Class and makes all the verbs and adjectives that connect to it use the prefixes for the Chi-Zi Class.

Chinyumba chachikulu chili pamenepajapo.   A giant house is over there.

This prefix is only used with some nouns.   Not everything can be 'magnified' using 'chi-'. Some words that do use 'chi-' are the following:

chinyumba	mansion, big house
chinjoka	giant snake
chigalu	big dog
chinyama	big animal
chimtengo	big tree, big stick
chimunthu	a giant; a crowd

Kutauni kunali chimunthu. There was a huge crowd in town.
Davide anapha chimunthu chachikulu. David killed a huge giant.

Sometimes 'chi-' conveys the idea of 'grotesque,' 'repulsive' or 'strange,' 'unrealistic':

thupi – body

chithupi – corpse (derogatory) (in the right context, it could also mean 'huge body')

chinyama – monster

Chapter 36: Nouns from Verbs

Earlier we learned about verbal adjectives, which enable us to say things like 'woyendetsa galimoto' which means 'driver' or 'wophunzira' which means 'student.' But there are a lot of verbs that have more direct ways of actually changing into a noun.

Some verbs just add the prefix 'm-' to name a person who does what the verb describes:

kubusa	>	mbusa
to herd animals		shepherd, goat herder, now also pastor

Some verbs add 'm-' and also change the last '-a' on the verb to '-i':

kuphunzitsa	>	mphunzitsi
to teach		teacher

When you do not want to make the verb into a 'person' noun but rather a 'thing' noun other changes can occur. For example, some verbs add 'chi-' on the front and change the final '-a' to '-o'.

kuzindikira	>	chizindikiro
to realize, to know		a sign, indication

Other words merely take the verb stem, add nothing in front, but replace the final '-a' with '-o'.

kuyankha	>	yankho\mayankho
to answer		answer

In changing verbs to nouns there are some definite patterns to observe, but notice that each word has to be learned on its own because there are so many variations.

People

kuphunzitsa	>	mphunzitsi\aphunzitsi
to teach		teacher
kukonza	>	mkonzi\akonzi
to repair,prepare,edit		editor, repairer
kubusa	>	mbusa\abusa
to herd animals		shepherd, herdsman, pastor
kunenera	>	mneneri\aneneri
to speak for someone		prophet, representative

Things

kuphunzira	>	phunziro\maphunziro
to learn		lesson
kuphunzitsa	>	chiphunzitso\ziphunzitso
to teach		teaching, doctrine
kuchita	>	mchitidwe
to do		action, way of acting

Note: look out for -dwe endings and notice how they are all
used to mean 'way of doing...'

kuoneka	>	maonekedwe
to appear, be visible		appearance
kuyenda	>	kayendedwe\mayendedwe
to travel, walk		way of going, means of travel
kuvina	>	kavinidwe\mavinidwe
to dance		way of dancing, dance style
kunena	>	kanenedwe\manenedwe
to say		pronunciation, way of speaking
kutchula	>	katchulidwe\matchulidwe
to name, state		pronunciation

197

kukonza	>	chikonzedwe
to repair, prepare		plan, idea, purpose
kuimba	>	kaimbidwe
to sing		way of singing
kukhala	>	khalidwe\makhalidwe
to be, live, stay		character, way one is
	>	chikhalidwe
		custom, manner
kufunsa	>	funso\mafunso
to ask		question
kuganiza	>	ganizo\maganizo
to think		thought, mind
	>	chiganizo\ziganizo
		sentence
kugaŵa	>	gaŵo\magaŵo
to divide, share		a division, part, share
kulira	>	maliro
to cry		funeral, mourning
kupembedza	>	chipembedzo\zipembedzo
to worship		religion, denomination
kupikisana	>	mpikisano\mipikisano
to compete, race		competition, race
kudziŵitsa	>	chidziŵitso
to let one know		knowledge
kusankha	>	chisankho
to choose		choice, election
kusankha	>	tsankho
to choose		prejudice
kunyansa	>	nyansi
to be disgusting, filthy		something nasty, filthy
kumvana	>	mvano
to agree		league, union of people

kuŵaula	>	mbaula
to roast over fire		charcoal brazier
kudula	>	njira yachidule
to cut off		shortcut
kudala	>	dalo\madalo
to be blessed		blessing
kudalitsa	>	dalitso\madalitso
to bless		blessing
kuphika	>	mphika\miphika
to cook		cooking pot
kubowola	>	mbowo\mibowo
to pierce a hole		hole
kuchiritsa	>	machiritso
to heal		healing
kulonjeza	>	lonjezo\malonjezo
to promise		promise
kulota	>	loto\maloto
to dream		dream
kulamula	>	lamulo\malamulo
to command, rule		law
	>	ulamuliro
		authority

Mwana wangayu amakonda ulimi. This child of mine likes
agriculture.
Kodi kwenikweni ulimi womwe amaukonda kwambiri ndi
wotani? Really, the agriculture that he likes a lot is what
kind?
Ulimi wamasamba ndi tomato ndi womwe amaukonda
kwambiri. Tomatoes and greens are what he likes to grow.
Mwana wanga ndi mlimi. My child is a farmer.

Chapter 37: Chi...re(ni)

Adding a 'chi-' prefix and a '-re' or '-reni' suffix to a verb can give it the idea of 'since...' Using the form as an adverb or adjective can introduce the idea of 'still,' or 'always'.

'Since'

Chibwerere kuno ku Zomba... Since coming here to Zomba...
Chipitireni ndakhala miyezi iŵiri. It's been two months since I went.
Chidzukire sindinasambe. Since waking up I haven't bathed.
Chidwalireni malungo aja sindikuthanso kumva bwinobwino. Ever since being sick with that malaria I haven't been able to hear properly.

'Still, always'

Chinthu chachidziŵikire. An obvious/well-known thing.
Akhala chiimire kwa maora ambiri. He's been continuously standing for many hours.
Ali chigonere pa mphasa. She's still lying on a mat.
(mphasa\mphasa – mat)

'Chikhalire' can mean 'eternal, having no beginning'
Mulungu ndi wachikhalire. God is eternal.
Nkhalangoyi ndi yachikhalire. This forest has always been around.
Madala akhala akupanga zimenezi kwachikhalire. Dad's been doing these things all along, forever.
'Wachikhalire' differs from 'wamuyaya' in that 'muyaya' speaks of future eternity, whereas 'chikhalire' looks at the past, having no beginning.

200

Chapter 38: Numbers

First, we'll look at the part of the old Chicheŵa number system that is still in common use, which is very small indeed. Secondly, we'll look at the modern number system, which is really just English numbers fit into Chicheŵa pronunciation. It is much more universally used.

The Old Number System

The numbers one through five are:
-modzi
-ŵiri
-tatu
-nayi
-sanu

These must be used with the verb prefixes.
Chinthu chimodzi.   One thing.
Anthu aŵiri. Two people.
Zinthu zitatu. Three things.
Tiagalu tinayi. Four little doggies.
Mazira asanu. Five eggs.

Important exception: Mu-A singular (munthu, etc.) puts an m- on the front of -modzi.
munthu mmodzi – one person
mwana mmodzi – one child
bambo mmodzi – one man, father
galu mmodzi – one dog
But plural is normal:
anthu aŵiri – two people

anthu amodzi – one people, a unified people

Other classes, as expected:
chinthu chimodzi – one thing
mpeni umodzi – one knife
njinga imodzi – one bicycle

The word for 'ten' is also still used, but rarely.
khumi – ten
chakhumi – tenth, tithe

Modern Numbers

As I said above, the old number system is now mainly used only for counting things up to five. For yourself at this point, you can primarily use the modern system, which is basically just the English numbers with Chicheŵa pronunciation. It is almost universally used for numbers higher than five.

Munthu wani.   One person.
Anthu thu.   Two people.
Anthu firi.   Three people.
Anthu folo.   Four people.

Faifi (5), sikisi (6), seveni (7), eyiti (8), naini (9), teni (10), leveni (11), twelofu (12), setini (13), fotini (14), fifitini (15), sikisitini (16), eyitini (18), naintini (19), twente (20), twente-wani (21), sate (30), fote (40), thu handredi (200), firi sauzande (3,000), etc.

Since there are no prefixes used, all the classes work with the modern number words in the same way:
Anthu faifi, zinthu faifi, mabuku faifi, etc.

Using Numbers

'Kukwana' (to amount to) is often the verb that gets used when you want to say how many of something there are.

Anthu anakwana angati? How many people were there?
Zingwe zinakwana zisanu. There were five strings.
Ndalama zakwana bwanji? How much money is there?

Alipo, pali, kuli, etc., are also commonly used:
Anthu alipo angati? How many people are there?
Alipo faifi. There are five.
Kuli mabuku angati? How many books are there?
Kuli mabuku thu handredi. There are two hundred books.
Padzakhala anthu awîri. There will be two people.

Note:
Words with a singular form can have a plural meaning and can still be counted:
> buledi muŵiri – two loaves of bread
> moŵa uŵiri – two beers

And plural forms can sometimes be 'one' if context demands:
> mafuta amodzi – one unit of oil
> mawu amodzi – one word
> Tonse ndife amodzi. We are all one/unified.

First, Second, Third...

'First' takes the verbal adjective form of 'kuyamba':
chinthu choyamba – the first thing
Adamu anali munthu woyamba. Adam was the first person.

From 'second' onward, an infix -chi- is used after the prefix
on the number word:
'Second' : Chinthu chachiŵiri, munthu wachiŵiri, nyimbo
yachiŵiri
'Third' : Chinthu chachitatu, munthu wachitatu
'Fourth' : Munthu wachinayi
'Fifth' : Tsiku lachisanu

For saying 'first,' 'second,' etc., with the modern/English
numbers, use the adjective prefix alone:
'Fifth': Munthu wafaifi
'Sixth': Chinthu chasikisi
'99th': Nyumba ya nainti-naini

Be careful not to confuse the following forms:
Zinthu sikisi – six things
Chinthu chasikisi – the sixth thing

Days of the week
The days Tuesday to Friday are merely named by their
number, counting as though Monday were the first day.
Note that all the names of the days have a prefix 'la-' as the
word 'tsiku' – 'day' is being referred to.
Lamulungu – Sunday (the day of God)
Lolemba – Monday (the day of 'writing', hiring)
Lachiŵiri – Tuesday (second day)
Lachitatu – Wednesday (third day)
Lachinayi – Thursday (fourth day)
Lachisanu – Friday (fifth day)
Loŵeruka – Saturday (the day of 'knocking off', going
home from work)

204

Once, twice, thrice, four times, etc.
These forms are shown by the prefix ka- on the number stem.
Kamodzi – once   Ndinapita kuBlantyre kamodzi. I went to Blantyre once.
Kaŵiri, katatu, kanayi, etc.

To use English numbers, it's the same:
Kafolo – four times
Katwenti-naini – 29 times

First time, second time, third time...
First time – koyamba
Second time – kachiŵiri
Kachitatu, kachinayi, etc.

-ngapo
While I'm on numbers, I might as well mention a very useful word, -ngapo.   It means something like 'several' or 'an unspecified number'.
Anthu angapo.   Several people.
Malo angapo.   Several places.
Mawiki angapo. Several weeks.
Nyemba zingapo. Several beans.
Minda ingapo. Several gardens.
Ndinapita kangapo. I went several times.

Pamodzi, Limodzi – together
Both of these words mean 'together'.
Ndinapita ku Blantyre pamodzi ndi Bile.
Ndinapita ku Blantyre limodzi ndi Bile.
I went to Blantyre together with Billy.

If a verb comes right before 'pamodzi/limodzi' it often takes
a -ra ending.
Tinapitira limodzi nawo. We went together with them.

'Ndi' often follows as in the examples above.
Joni anadyera pamodzi ndi ife. John ate together with us.

Pakati pa antchito apano, pali munthu mmodzi amene ndi
wokhulupirika.
Among the workers (antchito) here, there is one person who
is reliable.

Ndinapita ku Mzuzu kamodzi kokha.
I went to Mzuzu only once.

Ulendo wachiŵiri ndidzafuna kuyenderanso Chitipa.
[On] the second trip I will want to visit Chitipa also.

Kuchikwati kunabwera anthu okwana faifi handredi.
Five hundred people came to the wedding.

Kapenanso anthu angapo sanabwere chifukwa cha
msonkhano wazandale.
Maybe also some people didn't come because of the
political meeting (meeting of political things [ndale
– politics]).

Choyamba, tikambirane za ndalama zapachikwati.
First let's discuss about the money for the wedding.

Ndimadyera limodzi ndi MacDonald.
I eat together with MacDonald.

Pakati pa anthu onse omwe anabwera kutchalitchi, Wongani
ndi yekhayo anapereka chakhumi.
Of all the people who came to church, Wongani is the only
one who gave a tithe/tenth.

M'banja lathu tinabadwa ana faifi, ine wachitatu.
In our family we were born five children, I [being] the third.

Chapter 39: Kuti

This little verb is extremely common and important to many different constructions and ideas.

a. Its basic meaning is 'to say.'
Akuti chiyani? What is he saying?
Akuti, 'Sindibwera.' He is saying, 'I won't come.'
Nkhuku zimati chiyani? What do chickens say?

Even though its form is similar to -li, which is very restricted as to which tenses can be used with it, -ti can be used with many different tenses and forms:
Ati... He has said...
Zimati... They (zinthu) say...
Sichingoti... It (chinthu) doesn't just say...
Adzati... They will say...

b. It can be used to mean 'think, intend, purpose, imagine.'
Ndimati ndibwere. I was thinking I should come.
Tinati sabwera ameneyu. We thought this one wouldn't come.
Anati mwina idzagwa mvula. He thought maybe it would rain.
Zimene mumati mugule ndi ziti? What are the things you were planning on buying?

c. 'Kuti' is often used to mean 'that'.
Anandiuza kuti sali bwino. He told me that he wasn't fine.

Note the difference between 'ngati' (if, as if, as though) and 'kuti' (that).

Anaona kuti mvula ikubwera. He saw that rain was coming.
(And it really was.)

Anaona ngati mvula ikubwera.   He thought rain was
coming. (Maybe it wasn't.)

Izi zikuonetsa kuti zili bwino. These show that they are
good. (They really are.)

Izi zikuonetsa ngati zili bwino. These show that they are
good. (Maybe they aren't.)

Chakuti, wakuti, yakuti...

Amakamba nkhani yakuti mvula ibwera yambiri.
He was talking about the subject *that* the rain would come
well.

Sanabwere pachifukwa chakuti amadwala.
He didn't come for the reason that he was sick.

Akuba amabwera nthaŵi yakuti aliyense amakhala atagona.
Thieves come at the time when everyone is usually asleep.

The -akuti forms above can be shortened to -oti (woti, choti,
yoti, zoti, etc.) with no change in meaning.

Apeza mwamuna woti alibe chikhalidwe. She's found a
husband who doesn't have character.

Izi ndi zingwe zoti n'zosapangidwa bwino. These are
strings that aren't made well.

Chakuti, wakuti, zakuti, lakuti, etc. can also indicate 'a
certain...,' 'so and so,' 'such and such'.

Ati anaona munthu wakuti. He said he saw a certain guy/
such and such a guy.

d. 'Pakuti' means 'since,' 'for,' 'because.'

Anapita ku Blantyre pakuti kumeneko kunali alamu ake.
He went to Blantyre since his in-law (respectful) was there.
(Mlamu\alamu – brother or sister of one's wife or husband)

e. 'Kwakuti,' 'mwakuti' can take the meaning 'such that.'

Ndinkadwala kwambiri mwakuti nthaŵi zina sindimathanso kuona bwino.
I used to be sick a lot, such that sometimes I couldn't even see well.

f. 'Koti, moti, poti' – 'such that, since'

Ndili bwino kwambiri koti sindikumvanso kupweteka kwina kulikonse.
I am very fine, such that I don't feel any more pain.
Kumudzi kwavuta kwambiri moti mvula sinagwe bwino chaka chatha.
At the the village there is great trouble since the rains did not fall well last year.

g. 'Osati' – 'not'

Tikuphunzira Chicheŵa, osati Chingerezi. We are learning Chicheŵa, not English.
Muzithamanga, osati chifukwa chakuti kuthamanga n'kokoma, koma chifukwa choti kumalimbitsa thupi. You should run, not because running feels good, but because it strengthens the body.

❖ ❖ ❖

Ndikudziŵa kuti anthu aŵa alibe ndalama.
I know that these people have no money.
Poyankha, abambo anati, 'Ayi.'
Answering, father said, 'No.'
Ndimati ndipite kwa mfumu.
I was thinking of going to the chief's.
Kumeneko mukanena kuti chiyani?
What are you going to say there?
Ndikapemphako ndalama.
I will go ask for money.
Ndipatseni madzi, osati Fanta.
Give me water, not Fanta.
Fanta sandithandiza mwakuti amangondiŵaŵitsa m'mimba.
Fanta doesn't help me since it just makes my stomach hurt.
(kuŵaŵa – to hurt, pain, be bitter; kuŵaŵitsa – causative of
kuŵaŵa)
Kukampani kumeneko akufuna anthu akuti anagwirapo
ntchito kwa zaka faifi. At that company they want people
who already worked for five years (have five years' work
experience).
Zimenezi ndi zinthu zoti ndilibe nazo chidwi.
These things are such that I have no interest in them.
(chidwi – interest, curiosity)

Chapter 40: Kutero and Kutere

These two verbs are special verbs in that they don't end with -a but with other vowels. These two verbs cannot be used with the 'verb changers' -ra, -tsa, -ka, etc., but can be used with most tenses. The first one, 'kutero,' means roughly, 'to do *that*,' while it's fellow, 'kutere,' means 'to do *this*.'

Kutero – be that, do that, say that, be like that, do like that, say like that

Kodi mwaona m'mene akuchitira paja? Nafenso nthaŵi ina tinatero.
Have you seen the way he's doing that there? We also at one time did like that.

Ine ndimalankhula mwa pang'onopang'ono. John satero. I speak slowly. John doesn't do that.

Yakobo sanatero konse! Jacob didn't say that at all!

As an adjective or adverb:
Nkhuku zotero ndi zomwe ndikufuna. Chickens like that are what I want.

Akayenda motero asochera. If they travel that route/in that way, they will get lost.

Zabwino zili kuti? Zotero n'zosoŵa kwambiri! Where are the good things? Such are very rare!

Kutere – be this, do this, say this, be like this, do like this, say like this

Zinthu zikutere. Things are going/working like this.

Titere. Let's do this.

Titatere, tamaliza basi. After doing like this, we are completely done.

212

As an adjective or adverb:

Moyo wotere ndi wabwino. Such a life as this is good.

Nyumba yanga idzakhala yotere. My house will be like this.

Kotero kuti… 'such that' or 'so'

Ndimamuona kaŵirikaŵiri, kotero kuti sindidzathanso kumuiwala moyo wanga wonse. I see him often, such that I won't ever be able to forget him all my life.

'Cha-': Direction

Often when **direction or orientation** of movement is in view, the prefix 'cha-', will be used along with 'ku' or the direction word.

Anapita kumaŵa. He went to the east. (maŵa – morning, east)

Anapita chakumaŵa. He went toward the east.

Nkhano zimayenda chakumbali. Crabs go sideways. (nkhano – crab)

Anandiyang'ana cham'mbali. He looked at me sideways. (kuyang'ana – to look at)

Mwana akuyenda chokwaŵa. The child is moving in a crawling manner. (Multisyllable verbs take 'cho-' rather than 'cha-' just like verbal adjectives.)

Pagule wao, anthuŵa amayenda chogwada. In their dance, these people move along squatting down. (gule – dance; kugwada – to squat, bow)

Even when the verb is not actually a 'motion' verb, the 'cha' particle can be used:

Mwana akugona chafufumimba. The child is sleeping on its stomach.

Mwana akugona chagada. The child is sleeping on its

back.

Sometimes there's not much practical difference if you leave it out.
Anayang'ana chakumwamba.   He looked upwards.
Anayang'ana kumwamba. He looked up.

Chapter 41: Using Chicheŵa

A proper look at the more idiomatic and colorful ways of speaking in Chicheŵa is impossible in a single small chapter. I will let the language speak for itself as I give you some examples of a few colorful expressions and proverbs.

Expressions, Euphemisms – Mau obisa, Mikulu-wiko

If you are an on-the-ground learner, you will pick up a lot of informal and colloquial expressions. This is an important part of the language learning process and you should try to make your speech as 'colloquial' as possible. Of course, be sure you know how and when to use an expression before doing so!

Learning how to say things 'the way they say them' is one of the keys to feeling less like an 'outsider' and having more meaningful and enjoyable communications with Chicheŵa speakers.

Pay attention to how people express themselves, what makes them laugh, how they tell jokes and how they express their emotions and feelings.

Expression	English	Normal Word	English
kutisiya	to leave us	kumwalira	to die
kuzisaka	to hunt them (ndalama)	----	to look for money, do business
kuthamanga-thamanga	to run around	----	to look for money, do business
kuchira	to get well	kubereka	to give birth

kuuma	to be dry	kusabereka	to be unable to bear children
wamtali zala	of long fingers	wakuba	thief
kuyendera chidendene	to walk on the heel	kunyada	to be proud
mpondamatiki	one who tramples on money	munthu wolemera	rich person
kutsamira mkono	to lean on one's arm	kumwalira	to die
kudzala chinangwa	to plant cassava	kumwalira	to die
kubisala pachipande	to hide behind the nsima spoon	kunama	to lie
mbiyang'ambe	beer pot breaker	chidakwa	drunkard
kuthima	to be extinguished	kuledzera	to be drunk
kukhala ndi pakati	to have in between	----	to be pregnant
kuyembekezera	to wait for, expect	----	to be pregnant
kukhala ndi mimba	to have a stomach	----	to be pregnant
kutopa	to be tired	----	to be pregnant
kuthiridwa mchenga m'maso	to have sand poured in the eyes	kupusitsidwa	to be tricked, deceived
zangandiŵamba	I will roast my own things	munthu womana	a stingy person
galu wakuda	black dog	njala	hunger, famine
kumeta	to shave hair	kuvinidwa chinamwali	to go through traditional initiation
mudzi	village	manda	grave
dziko	country, world	manda	grave
kutemetsa nkhwangwa pa mwala	to strike the rock with the axe	kunenetsa	to say something in a strong way

216

Proverbs – Miyambi

Chicheŵa proverbs are summaries or conclusions from a traditional story (nthano) teaching an important lesson. Find someone to tell you the story for each proverb listed below.

Chakudza sichiimba ng'oma.
What comes doesn't play the drum. One is never ready for the trouble that comes his way.

Kanthu ndi khama, phwiti adakwata njiŵa.
Anything with diligence, even the sparrow married the dove.

Ali dere nkulinga utayenda naye.
To say someone is a certain way means you have walked with him.

Apatsa mosiyana.
God blesses people differently.

Choipa chitsata mwini.
Evil pursues its owner, the one who started it.

Chikomekome cha nkhuyu m'kati muli nyerere.
With all the good looks of the fig, inside there are ants.
Good appearances can be deceiving.

Chosamva adachiphikira m'masamba.
The insect that didn't listen got cooked together with the greens. Listen to warnings.

Ukakwera pamsana panjovu, usamati kunja kulibe mame.
When you are riding on an elephant, don't say that there is no dew elsewhere. If you are enjoying prosperity don't think that others aren't going through trials.

Linda madzi apite ndiye udziti ndadala.
Wait for the water to pass then say 'I'm blessed.' Don't boast in great achievements when you haven't yet

accomplished them.

Ukaipa dziŵa nyimbo.
When you seem the worst in the group, 'know a song.'

Khwangwala wamantha adafa ndi ukalamba.
The fearful crow died of old age. Prevention is better than cure.

Chisoni chidapha nkhwali.
Compassion killed the quail. Be careful who you have compassion on.

Atambwali sametana.
Crooks don't cut each others' hair.

Ichi chakoma, ichi chakoma, pusi adagwa chagada.
This is good! This is good! The monkey fell on his back. Wanting many things at once will put you in trouble.

Lende n'kukankhana.
A swing is for pushing each other. We should help each other in trouble.

Pendapenda sikugwa koma kuchalira ulendo.
Staggering is not falling but getting ready for the journey.

Safunsa adadya phula.
The one who didn't ask ate the wax.

Sapalamula adakhalira mazira amfumu.
The one who wanted to do nothing wrong sat in the chief's eggs. You can't ever stay completely out of trouble.

Walira mvula walira matope.
If you have cried for rain you have cried for mud.

Wakwatira kwamphezi saopa kung'anima.
He who married the daughter of lightning isn't afraid of flashing light.

218

Tsabola wakale saŵaŵa.
Old chilis aren't hot. We need new wisdom for the modern situation.

Mau a akulu akoma akagonera.
The words of older people are sweet where they fall. We should listen to the elders.

Modern Influences

The environment in which Chicheŵa is spoken has gone through some important changes in the last hundred years or so, and this has brought a corresponding change in the language itself. Originally Chicheŵa served a largely rural and agrarian society, with a huge weight of vocabulary in words specific to the village, garden, bush, hunt, dance and hand craft. Now, although the village still hosts a large proportion of Chicheŵa speakers, cultural interest is shifting somewhat from those categories due to modern influences.

Many 'language makers', such as people in the media and arts are bringing new influences into the Chicheŵa world. City life and culture are encroaching on the traditional, and traditional lifestyles and values are sometimes dropped in favour of Western ones. More and more Malaŵians are growing up in town with only minimal exposure to their cultural roots. When a large number of young people in this condition are brought up together in town or in boarding schools, this loss of traditional Cheŵa-ness is no longer a personal issue but becomes a social one, with now a new society being formed of people who are more or less distant from their cultural roots, and from the people whose lives are still shaped by that culture. Another factor comes into play even when young people have some interaction with 'the village' but they feel that it is inferior to the glamorous and exciting world of technology and materialism.

This lack of interest in Chicheŵa language and culture leads to a merely utilitarian use of it, and, where such is the case, the more beautiful and artistic elements of the language are at risk of being lost all together.

Words like *ng'anjo* (iron-smelting furnace) and *nguwo* (handmade skirt) are all but completely forgotten and only preserved in ancient sayings that many don't understand anymore. Even some basic vocabulary is being threatened by a similar trend. The widespread loss of the older generation due to health factors and the cultivation of youth subcultures accelerates the linguistic loss as words like '*bo*' (from Portuguese '*bom*') replace '*bwino*' and '*kuvaya*' (maybe from English 'via' or Portuguesse '*vai*') replaces '*kupita*'. Like many indigenous languages, Chicheŵa is changing due to its changing environment.

This element of change in Chicheŵa is a very important factor. More educated people tend to use Chicheŵa for chatting but English for formal conversation because of the drift of the language into imprecision. Especially young city people tend to develop their own new ways of speaking. Those in rural areas, and older people everywhere, find it harder to communicate with their urban or younger counterparts.

Unfortunately, your colloquial acquisitions might include some slang and substandard usage. Learning how to use a certain amount of modern 'lingo' is not necessarily a bad thing, but you will want to be able to use a 'pure' Chicheŵa as a general rule. Try to speak the very best Chicheŵa possible. When you learn a new colloquial phrase and are not sure how to categorize it in your mind, feel free to ask about how and where to use it.

220

Some Modern Slang:

You wouldn't want to use any of these at a funeral or village court hearing! Also realize that much modern slang is very restricted to certain areas or groups of people.

bo – good
shapu – hi
kuvaya – to go
kuphanda – to read
kujoyina – to join
kunjoya – to enjoy
phaks – food
memo – food
kushauwa – to 'chow', eat
mesho – roommate
deni – home
geri – school

Made in the USA
Lexington, KY
27 December 2014